SOUTHERN
CASSEROLES

WITHDRAWN

FROM COLLECTION

Southern Casseroles

COMFORTING POT-LUCKY DISHES

DENISE GEE

Photographs by Robert M. Peacock

CHRONICLE BOOKS

SAN FRANCISCO

Library of Congress Cataloging-in-Publication Data available.
ISBN: 978-1-4521-1228-2

Manufactured in China

Designed by Supriya Kalidas
Food and prop styling by Denise Gee

10 9 8 7 6 5 4 3 2 1

Chronicle Books LLC
680 Second Street
San Francisco, California 94107
www.chroniclebooks.com

DEDICATION

To my sweet brother and sister-in-law,
DEMPSE & ANNE McMULLEN,
whose comforting home, food,
and generous spirit are always
nourishment for the soul.

ACKNOWLEDGMENTS

To my literary agent extraordinaire, **ANGELA MILLER**, for championing the art of storytelling.

To **BILL LEBLOND** and **AMY TREADWELL**, for believing in my voice and vision. And for **SUPRIYA KALIDAS** for guiding my creative spirit—and love of good food— in such a cool and stylish way.

To **REBECCA SHERMAN**, for always being there to help me get my publishing projects not just up on their feet, but running.

To **JOY & KIRK KIRKSEY**, for sharing some cool casserole wares for photography.

And to my husband, **ROBERT PEACOCK**, whose love of food and family truly shines.

CONTENTS

> "Table looks almost too pretty to be molested!" Uncle Noah Webster hollered from the foot, sitting high on the sugar barrel. Granny's table was seated 'round with her grandchildren. . . . "You brought your chicken pie," Miss Beulah said, relieving her of the apron-covered dishpan. "And Jack's exactly who I made it for," said Aunt Beck. "If I made my good chicken pie, he'll come eat it, I thought, every dusty mile of the way."
>
> **EUDORA WELTY**, LOSING BATTLES (1970) / *When Miss Eudora was reminded of this passage while being interviewed for* A Cook's Tour of Mississippi *(see page 107), she said of that chicken pie, "I always heard it was a Methodist dish."*

One of my earliest memories from girlhood in Natchez, Mississippi, is watching my grandmother clean the kitchen counter around her Thermador double-oven range with six gas burners, a nearly commercial-grade unit that amazes me now in its uniqueness. Most of my friends' houses had the usual oven and range setup. Not ours. Nannie liked to cook, selling her jellies and jams all over the world (with Bob Hope and Lucille Ball being fans). That was quite a feat before the Internet. Her cooking prowess was recognized through word of mouth, which says a lot. So did her cooking style.

Nannie was usually cleaning the area from having just put together the night's meal—a casserole of some sort, one sitting in the oven, about to do its thing. The aromas of a little garlic or smothered chicken and onions or wild rice or shrimp were woo-worthy. I'd stare through the oven's glass door, watching ingredients bubble and steam as they came together in three- or four- or five-part harmony. Sometimes the casserole was put together from scratch; other times,

when time or temperament was short, it resulted from a can of this, a pound of that, a few dashes of this, and imagine that. Whatever it was, it had to rest a while before we could dig in. Salads were made—almost always wedges of iceberg with homemade blue cheese or green goddess dressing. In those cases, if the casserole was fairly self-contained, we'd put it all on one plate and have at it, but if the casserole risked becoming one with the salad, we'd use one of the many gratin dishes kept stacked in the cupboard. If, on the other hand, the casserole was a good mix of vegetables and protein—think chicken pot pie—yet challenging to eat on a flat surface, we often grabbed any number of blue-and-white soup plates to beautifully cradle the hearty mix. Buttery garlic bread was the last to come out of the oven: a slice of that would be plopped atop the plate, and off we'd head to the dining room or, if *All in the Family* was on, to sit in the TV room with the Bunker clan of Queens, whose accents and actions seemed almost exotic in our part of the world.

Inspired by the acclaimed cookbooks of my cousin, entertaining and design guru Lee Bailey, as well as my grandmother's own homespun cookbooks, I ultimately became a food editor at *Southern Living* magazine. It was there that I tasted almost every casserole known to man—often as many as twelve in a day whenever a big story or contest warranted. At the time, most of us were trying to get away from our "Becky Home-Ec-ky" reputation, much to the chagrin of some elder editors, and many of us were courting chefs for more inventive recipes to feature. But to my own chagrin, whenever I'd leave the South for a meeting or event, one of the first things mentioned would be our region's love of casseroles—primarily of our fondness of one ingredient: "How can you stand to eat all that creamed soup?" I developed a defense mechanism, always replying that I didn't share that fondness. But I was a hypocrite. Whenever I craved a taste of home, invariably I'd make a casserole, one that sometimes harbored said cream of mushroom or celery soup—despite knowing, as Nannie knew, how to make a basic white sauce or tomato sauce and create a dish from the ground up.

After years of keeping my secret love of casseroles in check—despite the many times I could have been outed over my glee to see a green bean casserole—I found myself 1,000 miles away in Iowa. It was there that my Southernness, which I'd always squirreled away, along with the accent I'd fought early on to conceal, was put under the spotlight. I could be talking about the most inconsequential thing, but sometimes it seemed as if I were reading a poem by Eudora Welty. And whenever I'd make a dish for a potluck, invariably there'd be oohs and aahs, but soon I realized my friends weren't just being polite in saying, "What amazing flavor." They really meant it.

But it was while drinking mint juleps with Southern friend and *Better Homes and Gardens* colleague Paige Porter in our Des Moines home, with snow on the ground, that I realized that over time—and perhaps out of homesickness—I truly had embraced my Mississippi roots. It wasn't just OK to be Southern. It was actually kind of special. And that was nice. (Though I must admit, I still had my challenges. While our kitchen was being remodeled, I was once asked by a colleague if I needed to borrow a deep-fat fryer: "Don't you all make hushpuppies or something for dinner every night?" she asked.)

After my mother's death, my brother and I divvied up some of Nannie's kitchenware, which my mother had taken with her to retirement in Florida. At first I thought she'd taken them there out of spite—she didn't cook and knew we did. It was only after Mama's passing that I realized she'd wanted them for sentimental reasons.

Nannie's old Wagner Magnalite aluminum casserole pots and Le Creuset casseroles and ramekins, which had been boxed up for so many years, brought back many wonderful memories. I cherish them, as I do her recipes and my friends' recipes—especially the casseroles, which embody so much love and flavor and family in every bite. And now that I've dug my heels into Texas, I'm enjoying flavor to the nth degree. With this book, I aim to share the glory of the second coming of the casserole.

Seasoned with good storytelling and contemporary flavor, this casserole cookbook is intended to be THE source for the best Southern casseroles—from main dishes to sides to breakfast and dessert treats, which are scattered hither and yon, from Junior League cookbooks to recipe cards and scrapbooks or binders. With this book, now there's one central place for the best of the best.

So just what is a Southern casserole? To my mind, it's anything with at least five ingredients that needs to bake for at least thirty minutes to meld into cohesive goodness before being served right from its dish. And how might it differ from, say, a Northern casserole? Flavor. Personality in the mix of regional ingredients. A sweet, sentimental serving style. A good story attached.

The only things I won't allow into the casserole? Anything with cereal (though I know some of you are just fine with that addition and that's OK). Nor will I call anything "Wiggle." On those I draw the line.

Otherwise, you can consider these the must-try, must-keep casseroles based on my way of thinking and upbringing, ones guaranteed to be attractive, easy to prepare, home-tested, and much inquired about. The flavors are based on my love of, well, flavor—having been born in Texas and raised in Mississippi by family from north and south Louisiana. And they represent the go-to dishes I've enjoyed cooking, tasting, and collecting during my travels as a food, entertaining, and home-design editor at such magazines as *Southern Living*, *Coastal Living*, and *Better Homes and Gardens*.

The main thing to know is that making casseroles is like jazz: Learn the notes, then improvise, honey.

CHAPTER 01

On a 'Role

This much I know: Some of you like taking an orderly approach to casserole cooking, while many of you simply want to dump and stir. Some of you prefer making everything from scratch, while many of you covet your can openers. No matter your style, I'm all for it. Just as long as it tastes good. And good it will be if you understand a few things before setting out to make a fashionable and flavorful Southern casserole.

GOOD TO KNOW, THEN GOOD TO GO

1 GOOD TIMING / Based on my Dallas kitchen's simple gas oven, whatever cooking time your sleek new convection appliance or old clunker needs to get the job done may not align perfectly, but the cooking time will indeed be very close. Just keep an eye on things. Check the dish ten minutes before its suggested completion time to gauge its ETA.

2 GOOD PLACEMENT / Recipe times, and success rates, can vary greatly if you don't use the proper dish. If it's too shallow, your casserole will cook too quickly and be dry; if it's too deep, it won't cook evenly (meaning it'll be gooey in the middle). Follow the instructions first, then feel free to improvise once you understand the recipe.

3 GOOD TASTE / Adjust each casserole's seasonings to suit yourself. If you're not a fan of garlic, just cut back on what I suggest. (Or, if you're really not a fan, don't include it at all.) Some I know think green onions are spicy, and that's as far as they'll go to add snap to their dish. Others say bring on not one jalapeño but two serrano chiles. You just do what the common-sense fairy tells you in order to make *your* taste buds happy.

4 GOOD PLANNING / Most of these recipes can be made the night before; in fact, having a dish's flavors come together for at least four and up to eight hours in the refrigerator often improves it. And if a cheese or a crunchy topping is part of a dish, I'll let you know when those ingredients should be added (usually just before baking, so the food won't get mealy).

5 GOOD EATING / Leftovers can be kept tightly covered in the refrigerator for several days without having their flavor compromised, though seafood casseroles should be eaten within one or two days, if you catch my, well, its (aroma) drift.

6 GOOD FREEZING / Most of these recipes can be frozen (see "Just Chill," page 41, for more on that). If for some reason it's not advisable (i.e., if the sauce might separate and become watery), I'll be sure to note that. Also, leftovers that have been refrigerated a couple of days will not freeze well; their unraveling flavors and texture will disappoint once put to the deep-freeze test. I realize, however, that some of you won't care a lick about what I just said and will go ahead and do it anyway, swearing that it's just as good as the day you cooked it. I'm not here to judge—only offer guidelines. Oh, and some good recipes. But first things first.

The late and very great Southern cooking doyenne Edna Lewis once told me that always having a ham in the refrigerator was akin to keeping a little black dress on standby in your closet: With either, you'd be ready for anything. So, too, will your kitchen if you keep many of these core casserole ingredients on hand.

IN THE PANTRY

Baking ingredients: All-purpose flour, cornmeal, baking mix (i.e., Bisquick), cornbread mix, baking soda, baking powder

Bread crumbs: Soft seasoned/unseasoned and panko

Broths: Chicken, beef, and vegetable

Canned tuna (chunk light and solid white) **and chicken**

Cheese: Processed loaf (i.e., Velveeta)

Chiles: Diced green, sliced jalapeño

Grits: Quick-cooking (not instant) and stone-ground

Nuts: Pecans, sliced/slivered almonds

Oils: Olive, vegetable, peanut

Olives: Pimiento-stuffed green, black, olive mix

Pasta: Dried spaghetti, penne, elbow, fettuccine, others

Pasta sauces: Commercially made tomato, Alfredo, pesto

Rice: Long-, short-, wild-grains; quick-cooking couscous

Seasonings: Ground sea or kosher salt, peppercorns for grinding, Italian, Cajun (low sodium), seafood, chili powder, cayenne pepper

Soups: Canned cream of mushroom, celery, and chicken

Stuffing mix

Sweeteners: granulated and brown sugars, light sweeteners (Splenda and agave nectar are my faves)

Tomatoes: Whole, diced (flavored/plain), sauce, paste, stewed with peppers

Vegetables: Canned corn, green beans, vegetable mix; black, white (cannellini, great Northern), and pinto; black-eyed peas

Vinegars: Pepper, balsamic, red wine

Wine: Red and white

IN THE 'FRIDGE

Condiments: Mayonnaise, ketchup, Dijon mustard

Cheese: Cheddar, Mexican/Italian blends, freshly grated Parmesan

Citrus: Lemons, limes (see Artificial Intelligence, page 16)

Dairy: Butter, margarine, milk, half-and-half, cream, sour cream, cream cheese

Dough: Canned biscuits, pie crusts, puff pastry

Eggs

Garlic: Minced, pureed

Meat: Ham, bacon

Onions: Green, red, sweet, white

Potatoes: Russet, red (new)

Sauces: Hot, soy, Worcestershire

IN THE FREEZER

Casseroles, of course!

Dough: Garlic bread, dinner rolls, biscuits, pie crusts

Fruit

Meat/seafood: Chicken breasts, shrimp

Onion/celery/bell pepper mix (a.k.a. "the holy trinity," see Lil' Dish, page 145)

Vegetables: Corn, green peas, lima beans, spinach

ARTIFICIAL INTELLIGENCE: LEMONS AND LIMES

Bottled lemon and lime juices? Just say no to their shapely charms. Their strongly sour and artificial flavor doesn't even come close to the soft tart-sweet goodness of fresh citrus. You can buy the bottled similar-to-fresh juice (usually organic), and keep it refrigerated for a time. Or, of course, you can squeeze your own and keep it chilled or frozen. I often use specific ice trays to harbor one or two tablespoons of lemon and lime juice, then pop out what I need for a fresh fix. It thaws in no time.

WHY GO ORGANIC?

With more companies taking the organic high road, the cost of better-for-us fare is coming down while our awareness of its benefits is rising. (Though we Southerners have understood the beauty of harvesting fresh food from lush, healthy gardens for centuries.) For cost-cutting and/or mass-production reasons, many of the foods we eat have us ingesting traces of toxic and/or synthetic pesticides and fertilizers—insecticides, fungicides and herbicides, growth hormones, antibiotics, and genetic modifiers.

Organic foods, however, are minimally processed without all of the above "enhancements"—or artificial ingredients, preservatives, or irradiation. Here are five good reasons to embrace organic foods:

+ It's better for us (see above).

+ It's better for our animals and agriculture (see above).

+ It's better for the environment (by decreasing pollution levels from, say, synthetic materials that make their way into our water supply).

+ It's better for our local farmers, who in some cases are struggling to keep an age-old family business—and revered Southern foodway—alive.

+ It tastes better: It's fresher, more flavorful, and nutrient-rich.

If I had to suggest only one organic food for you to splurge on, I'd say go with organic dairy products—that is, unless savoring products from dairy cows treated with chemicals and milk that might be harboring antibiotics and bovine growth hormones, is just too darn yummy for you to resist. I'm just sayin'.

SPACE HEATERS / When it comes to the best baking dishes, glass, ceramic, cast-iron/enameled, and earthenware vessels are ideal for cooking casseroles, since they retain their heat long after you pull them from the oven. Yet with that in mind, they also heat slower than their metallic counterparts, so you might have to increase your cooking time by 20 to 30 percent. Although metal baking pans are good for creating a light crust, dark ones can dry out your casserole, and aluminum and cast-iron pans sometimes react with acidic foods like tomatoes, making them taste, well, tinnish, so save your cast-iron and enamelware pans for creamy, non-acidic recipes.

BY THE NUMBERS / If you don't have a specific casserole dish a recipe calls for, you often can use another pan if you know its equivalent volume. Dish dimensions make a difference in baking times—and affect whether or not to cover them (to preserve moistness in, say, a shallow dish). If you're unsure of your pan size (vintage ones are often unmarked), lay a ruler across the top and measure from inner edge to inner edge. Measure the depth from bottom to top. To determine volume, use a measuring cup to fill the pan with water. (Then, when you know what quart-size it is, write its measurements on the pan's bottom with an indelible marker for future reference).

IF THE RECIPE CALLS FOR A . . .	CONSIDER A . . .
1-quart dish (4 cups)	6-by-2-inch round pan 8-by-1.5-inch round pan 8-by-1.5-inch pie pan 4 (8-ounce) ramekins
1.5-quart dish (6 cups)	8-by-2-inch round pan 10-by-1.5-inch pie pan 8-by-8-by-1.5-inch square pan 11-by-7-by-2-inch rectangular pan 4 (12-ounce) or 6 (8-ounce) ramekins
2-quart dish (8 cups)	9-by-2-inch round pan 9-by-2-inch pie pan 8-by-8-by-2-inch square pan 9-by-9-by-1.5-inch square pan 8 (8-ounce) or 4 (16-ounce) ramekins
2.5-quart dish (10 cups)	9-by-9-by-2-inch square pan 8 (10-ounce) or 6 (14-ounce) ramekins
3-quart dish (12 cups)	9-by-3-inch round pan 10-by-10-by-2-inch square pan 13-by-9-by-2-inch rectangular pan 2 (8-by-8-by-2-inch) pans 8 (12-ounce) or 6 (16-ounce) ramekins

AT YOUR SERVICE

Having some basic casserole dishes on hand will speed things up:

+ 2- to 4-cup ramekins for appetizers

+ 1-quart dishes for smaller servings

+ Shallow casseroles in oval, rectangular, square, and other shapes for vessel variety and visual interest

+ Dutch ovens with lids (averaging 3 to 6 quarts) and round soufflé dishes (at least 2 quarts)

+ One each of 8-by-8-inch, 9-by-9-inch, 13-by-9-inch, and 9-by-2-inch and/or 9-by-3-inch round baking dishes

TOP TIPS

+ Make sure your dish is oven safe. This is very important to know before you stick it in the oven. Some artisan pans, or mass-produced dishes, if not marked "ovenproof," will shatter when heated to certain high temperatures; they also might contain lead. Ask the craftsperson or store owner, or inspect the box closely to see if it's safe for food and/or cooking—or if it's purely just kitchen decoration.

+ For fast cleanup, grease casserole pans or dishes with nonstick cooking spray.

+ Avoid cooking on top and bottom oven racks. The middle of the oven is where the most even heat should be centered.

+ Ovens heat differently, so check for doneness about 10 minutes before the minimum cooking time.

+ If you use aluminum foil to cover a casserole, place the shiny side down so it retains, instead of deflecting, the heat.

CHICKEN

For its versatility and ease of access, poultry is by far the most popular meat used in Southern casseroles. Roast or sauté your own or buy it cooked or packaged from the deli. (In a pinch, you can use canned, but you'll definitely need to liven it up with sauce and seasoning.)

+ 1 pound of bone-in uncooked chicken = about 1 cup cooked shredded/chopped chicken

+ One 12-ounce whole boneless, skinless breast = 1 cup cooked shredded/chopped chicken; a 6-ounce half-breast = ½ cup cooked shredded/chopped chicken

+ One 2- to 3-pound cooked rotisserie chicken = 3 to 4 cups cooked shredded/chopped chicken

+ 1 pound ground chicken = 2 to 2¼ cups cooked

Easy & Flavorful Chicken

MAKES 7–8 CUPS COOKED CHICKEN AND 8 CUPS FAT-SKIMMED STOCK

To give typically bland chicken pieces a home-cooked flavor, follow this recipe.
Cooking them bone-in will make the meat's flavor richer. This also will yield a nice stock.

5 to 6 pounds bone-in chicken breasts and, if desired, bone-in thighs

1 medium onion, quartered

3 celery stalks with tops, quartered

3 carrots, quartered

2 garlic cloves, halved

2 bay leaves

1 tablespoon ground sea or kosher salt

2 teaspoons ground black pepper

To an 8-quart or larger stockpot or Dutch oven, add 9 cups water, the chicken, onion, celery, carrots, garlic, bay leaves, salt, and pepper. Bring to a boil over medium heat, about 10 minutes. Cover, reduce the heat, and simmer for 30 to 40 minutes, or until the chicken is tender and a thermometer inserted into the thickest portion registers 160°F (the temperature will rise another 5 degrees before serving). Remove the chicken from the broth and let it cool slightly before attempting to remove and discard the skin and bones. If desired, strain, cool, and refrigerate the stock for other uses. Shred or chop the meat before using as directed.

Storage

In an airtight container wrapped in aluminum foil, cooked chicken will keep in the refrigerator for up to 4 days and in the freezer for up to 2 months. When freezing, separate chicken pieces, and, if desired, strained broth, into 1- or 2-cup portions placed into smaller bags or containers to be pulled out for future recipes. Strained broth will freeze well for several months.

MEATLESS

+ **TOFU /** Technically, it's sliceable bean curd. Actually, it's delicious if it can be prepared to be as flavorful and crunchy as possible. Cube and fry it in oil and seasoning for 4 to 6 minutes until it turns golden brown, or crisp it in a hot oven with a coating of soy sauce and other seasonings. One pound of tofu equals about 2 cups cooked.

+ **TEXTURED VEGETABLE BLENDS /** Chicken-style strips and meat- and sausage-style crumbles are excellent options for more healthful dining. One 12-ounce bag equates to about 1 pound ground beef or about 3 cups.

TURKEY

+ **GROUND /** This is a great choice for anyone watching fat intake, but it can taste like cardboard if it's unseasoned. Fortunately, you now can buy preseasoned ground turkey (I especially like the Italian-flavored variety), but be generous in seasoning it yourself if it's just plain ground turkey. 1 pound uncooked measures 2 to 2¼ cups cooked.

+ **BREAST /** I prefer to roast my own turkey breasts and shred them. One 5- to 7-pound fresh or frozen and thawed turkey breast should cook at 325°F for 2 to 3 hours or to its recommended internal temperature (see chart, facing page). There will be about 3 cups of cooked turkey per pound. Allow 8 ounces per person for generous portions and seconds or leftovers.

PORK

+ **HAM /** A fully cooked bone-in ham is flavorful and versatile. Buy them precooked boneless or bone-in, or cook a 7- to 8-pound bone-in ham at 325°F for 18 to 25 minutes per pound (1 pound equals about 3 cups diced). Diced offers the meatiest texture, but you also can also buy it pre-diced (but in smaller pieces) at the deli.

+ **LOIN ROASTS /** These can be found precooked (deliciously so at Mexican grocer delis), or you can cook your own. A 2- to 5-pound roast at 350°F takes 20 to 25 minutes per pound. As with any large cut of meat, cook to about 5 degrees shy of minimum cooking temperature and let it sit for 10 minutes (it will then rise to its ideal temperature). Two pounds of bone-in pork loin equals 1 pound (3 cups) cooked meat.

+ **SAUSAGE /** Cook ground sausage until it's browned through; drain it well before adding to your casserole. Precooked sausage alleviates temperature (and grease) worries. One pound sliced smoked sausage equals about 4 cups; bulk sausage or fattier links (e.g., chorizo) equal 3 to 3½ cups per pound.

BEEF & LAMB

+ **CHUCK ROAST /** Season a 3- to 4-pound roast to your liking, dust it lightly with all-purpose flour, then sear on all sides in a little oil in a large Dutch oven. Add about 4 cups of seasoned water (I sometimes use a packet of ranch dressing or onion soup mix stirred in) and cook it covered, over medium-low heat for 3 to 4 hours, turning occasionally, until tender and at its recommended internal temperature (see chart, facing page). (This same procedure can be adapted for an equal amount of chuck stew meat chunks.) One pound equals about 3 cups chopped or shredded.

NOTE: I don't advise cooking a less-tender rump roast for a casserole unless you cook it in a slow cooker forever and a day. (For more on using slow cookers, see Cooking Low & Slow, page 40.)

+ **GROUND /** Brown meat until it's cooked through and at its recommended internal temperature (see chart, facing page); drain it well before adding it to your casserole. One pound equals about 3½ cups.

SEAFOOD

In all cases, use fresh or flash-frozen and thawed, and know that seafood is fully cooked when no longer translucent at the center.

+ **SHRIMP /** Prepeeled, deveined, and uncooked are the best choices for ease and flavor. (Note that precooked shrimp are good for quick stir-fries, cocktails, or salads, but can get tough in casseroles.) Medium-size shrimp (41/50 count per pound) will be a bit sweeter and easier to eat; they also can be cooked right in the casserole. Canned shrimp, rinsed well, are OK for spreads and dips, but small fresh ones will taste less like a tin can.

+ **CRAWFISH /** Tails from the Gulf (which I prefer for reasons expressed in the "Lil' Dish" on page 61) are available in convenient 1-pound packages, while imported crawfish come in 12-ounce packets. The latter will always be cheaper, and since it appears close in size to the former, many will grab that smaller package and think they're getting a good deal. Once home, however, they'll realize they've actually just docked their casserole 4 ounces of precious cargo. So, read the label carefully to know what you're getting (or not getting).

+ **CATFISH NUGGETS /** These 1- to 2-inch-thick/wide pieces make the best choices for seafood casseroles, especially if they're flash-seared with a bit of seasoning before going into the dish.

+ **CRAB, OYSTERS /** They can be expensive, but they're so worth having in elegant dishes, particularly ones with light cream sauces that will enhance the delicate seafood instead of overpower it. The crème de la crème of crab is **jumbo lump**, which offers the biggest chunks (from the crab's two back swimming legs), whitest color, firmest texture, and sweetest taste. **Regular lump**, from the body cavity, is as sweet as jumbo lump but slightly smaller in size and not as vibrant white. **Claw meat** has a stronger flavor and spongier

texture. As for **canned crab**? I find it too briny, and once rinsed well to rectify that, it becomes too piecey. But it's usually fine for spreads and dips. Pints of freshly shucked oysters should be purchased from a reputable seafood shop and, like crabmeat, be kept very cold. Canned oysters (regular and smoked) are more affordable options for soups and stews.

+ **CANNED TUNA /** It should be firm and flaky, never mushy. It should be moist but not watery, and certainly not dry. I find springwater–enveloped chunk-light albacore or tongol the best looking and tasting.

   NOTE: I don't suggest using canned salmon for anything other than an emergency situation. I think it tastes down-right odd once you've had the fresh. (Sorry!)

Here are the USDA's minimum recommended internal temperatures for meats and poultry:

FOOD	MINIMUM INTERNAL TEMP
Fish, shellfish, lamb	145°F
Beef (whole cuts)	145°F
Pork, ham	145°F
Ground beef, sausage	160°F
Eggs	160°F
Poultry, stuffed meats	165°F

Let's start with the mother of all sauces: The basic white sauce, or "roux," as those along our Frenchified Gulf Coast call it. It would behoove you to commit it to memory, since it's the heart of four other essential sauces that follow the main recipe. For the freshest flavor, use Classic White, Mornay, or Cream of Mushroom sauce recipes in place of cream soup in any recipe calling for one 10.75-ounce can.

Classic White Sauce

MAKES ABOUT 1½ CUPS

¼ cup butter or vegetable oil (see Notes)

¼ cup all-purpose flour

1 cup whole milk, half-and-half, or cream, warm (see Notes)

½ teaspoon ground sea or kosher salt

¼ teaspoon ground white or black pepper (see Notes)

Dash of nutmeg

In a medium heavy-bottomed saucepan over medium-low heat, melt the butter and add the flour, whisking constantly until the mixture begins to bubble, 1 to 2 minutes. Slowly add the milk, and whisk to combine. When it just begins to boil, in about 2 minutes, reduce the heat to low, and whisk the sauce until smooth and thickened, 1 to 2 minutes. Season with the salt, pepper, and nutmeg. Use as directed.

Cream of Mushroom Sauce

MAKES ABOUT 1½ CUPS

Using the Classic White Sauce recipe, add ¾ cup finely chopped mushrooms to the butter and sauté until tender. Instead of milk, use beef broth.

Mornay Sauce

MAKES ABOUT 1½ CUPS

Using the Classic White Sauce recipe, add 1 medium shallot, minced, and 1 pressed garlic clove to the butter and sauté until tender. Increase the flour by 1 tablespoon (slightly less than ⅓ cup) and use 1¾ to 2 cups warm milk (to create desired consistency). Add ⅛ teaspoon nutmeg and ¼ cup freshly grated Gruyère, Parmesan, or white Cheddar cheese (ideally 3 tablespoons Gruyère and 1 tablespoon either Parmesan or white Cheddar).

Cheese Sauce

MAKES ABOUT 2½ CUPS

For traditional mac 'n' cheese, use the Classic White Sauce recipe and add another 1 cup warm milk (for 2 cups total), 1 cup shredded sharp Cheddar cheese, ⅛ teaspoon dry mustard, and, if desired, a pinch of cayenne pepper or dash of hot sauce. For more contemporary mac 'n' cheese or scalloped potatoes, use a cheese like Gruyère and omit the dry mustard.

Alfredo Sauce

∘— MAKES ABOUT 2¾ CUPS —∘

Using the Classic White Sauce recipe, omit the flour and instead add 8 ounces cream cheese and 1 cup freshly grated Parmesan cheese to the butter and milk. Heat over low heat, stirring often, for about 15 minutes, or until the sauce is well incorporated.

NOTES: Vegetable oil and white pepper are often used to ensure the whitest sauce (though the flavor is less buttery); use black pepper if desired.

Microwave each cup of milk for 40 to 50 seconds before adding it to the roux; warm milk (105°F to 110°F) will help the sauce incorporate faster and create less floury lumps. Without warming the milk, the sauce will be fine as long as you whisk it constantly; strain out any lumps if necessary.

The richer the dairy product, the richer the sauce.

For more complex flavor, replace half the liquid with chicken broth.

For a thinner sauce, reduce the butter and flour by half.

Storage

Cream-based sauces can be made ahead and stored in an airtight container in the refrigerator for several days. To prevent a skin from forming, lightly press plastic wrap or wax paper against the surface. Warm the sauce over low heat before using. As for freezing, I'm not a big fan; cream-based sauces tend to separate. Some of my friends swear it will freeze well for a couple of weeks, and that once it is mixed into a casserole and cheese is added, people never notice the difference. (Well, some people.) Defrost the sauce slowly in the refrigerator (overnight is best) and warm it in a sauce-pan over low heat, whisking in a little cold butter to help unify it.

◆ LIL' DISH ◆

STOCK MARKET

If you're a cook who makes stock from scratch and freezes it for use later, I worship at your feet. When a recipe calls for chicken or beef stock, I usually reach for one of the great organic ready-made broths on the market now. Boosted with mirepoix (vegetables), they're surprisingly flavorful. I've had great success with Swanson's Certified Organic Free Range Chicken Broth and Trader Joe's Free Range Chicken Broth. Bouillon cubes have come a long way, but the best is not a cube—it comes in a jar. Better Than Bouillon's concentrated paste food bases are made from meat, seafood, or vegetables, making them richer and better tasting than ordinary cubes. Available at most large supermarkets or online at SuperiorTouch.com, they also come in low-sodium, kosher, and vegan-certified varieties.

Go-to Marinara Sauce

MAKES ABOUT 4 CUPS

※

This is my go-to spaghetti sauce. For the best flavor, let the ingredients marry overnight
in the refrigerator before reheating either in a casserole or to serve atop pasta.
When time's short, I replace the basil, parsley, and oregano with Italian herb seasoning
blend from a grinder, available from McCormick at most large supermarkets. I often
double or triple this recipe and freeze part of it for later use (it freezes beautifully).
Brown sugar is best for balancing the sharp acidity of tomatoes (especially canned ones)
and enhancing their natural sweetness.

2 tablespoons olive oil or butter

½ cup finely diced onion

One 28-ounce can whole tomatoes, broken into pieces, with their juices, or about 2 pounds ripe, peeled tomatoes

One 6-ounce can tomato paste

¼ cup white wine or chicken broth

1 tablespoon chopped fresh or 1 teaspoon dried basil

1 tablespoon chopped fresh or 1 teaspoon dried flat-leaf Italian parsley (optional)

1½ teaspoons chopped fresh or ½ teaspoon dried oregano

1 teaspoon minced garlic

½ to 1 teaspoon ground sea or kosher salt

½ to 1 teaspoon ground black pepper

¼ to ½ teaspoon dried red pepper flakes (optional)

1 tablespoon brown or granulated sugar

In a Dutch oven, warm the olive oil and sauté the onion until tender, about 5 minutes.

Add the tomatoes and juices, tomato paste, wine, basil, parsley (if desired), oregano, garlic, salt, black pepper, and red pepper flakes (if desired). Stir well and let simmer for about 10 minutes.

Add the brown sugar and stir to combine well. Reduce the heat and let simmer for about 20 minutes, until the flavors meld. Adjust the seasonings as desired. Use as directed.

Storage

This will keep well in an airtight container in the refrigerator for about 1 week and in the freezer for 6 months. Use a zip-top plastic freezer bag, which lets you freeze it flat and save space. Thaw the sauce in the refrigerator or defrost it in the microwave before slowly reheating in a pot. See "Just Chill" (page 41) for more tips.

Rice is as Southern as grits, but it's decidedly more common nationally, and quite easy to cook. **Long-grain** is long and slender, with grains that separate well and stay fluffy, making it a stand-up choice for food bases or side dishes. **Medium-grain** is shorter and stouter, most often seen in risotto. **Short-grain** is round and moist, making it stick together when cooked in, say, rice pudding. **Brown** is dehusked, but its nutritious bran and germ are left intact, making it nuttier, chewier, healthier, and heftier (and it takes about twice as long to cook as white). **White** has been milled or "polished" a step further (to remove the bran and the germ), so it's whiter and softer (but because it lacks nutrients, it's often "enriched"). **Converted/parboiled** (precooked and dehydrated) is beige, but similar to enriched white rice in taste and texture. **Instant** is also precooked and dehydrated, but in the process of making it quicker to cook, flavor, texture, and nutrition are lost. (That, and it's more expensive!) Like instant grits, I don't suggest it. In just 15 minutes more of cooking time, you can have a far superior rice.

Wild rice isn't rice at all; it's grass seed similar to rice (mostly grown in the upper Midwest). Its nuttier flavor complements dark-meat poultry and game birds like duck and quail especially well, and its more elegant look has us adoring its use in dressings and side dishes meant for company.

KERNELS OF WISDOM

+ White rice can be stored in an airtight container in a cool, dry area of your pantry for about 1 year.

+ Brown rice goes rancid faster than white because of the bran's fatty oils and acids. To extend its shelf life, store it in an airtight container in the refrigerator for 5 to 6 months. Before cooking it, smell it to ensure it doesn't smell like old cooking oil.

+ For fluffy rice, remove the pot from the heat after cooking and let it sit undisturbed with the lid on for at least 5 minutes and up to 30 minutes.

+ To infuse your rice with more flavor, replace all or part of its water with chicken, beef, or vegetable broth, or use one part fruit juice (think orange or pineapple) or coconut milk to one part water.

+ To whiten rice and keep it from sticking, add a few drops of fresh lemon juice to the boiling water before adding the rice.

+ Cooked rice should stay in your refrigerator no more than 5 days. To freeze it, measure 1- or 2-cup portions of it atop plastic freezer wrap. Flatten it into a square and wrap tightly, marking the portion size. Lay it flat in the freezer

RICE	CUPS LIQUID PER 1 CUP RICE	MINUTES TO COOK
Basmati	2	18 to 20
Brown, long-grain	2½	40 to 45
Brown, medium-/short-grain	2¼	40 to 45
Carolina	1¾	18 to 20
Converted (parboiled)	2	25
Jasmine	2	18 to 20
Popcorn	1½	20 to 25
Texmati (Della)	2	18 to 20

and, when frozen, add all the squares to a large zip-top plastic freezer bag, where it will keep for about 6 months. To reheat the rice, unwrap a square and place it in a microwave-safe container with a lid. Add 1 teaspoon water for each 1 cup of rice and cook at 50 percent power for 1 to 1½ minutes. Using a fork, fluff up the rice and cook once more at the same power, if necessary, to reach the desired consistency and temperature.

LIL' DISH

TRUE SOUTHERN RICES

Nearly 85 percent of the rice Americans eat is grown in the South. Of those, these are my five favorite rice varieties unique to our region:

+ **CAROLINA /** One of the most popular long-grain rices in the United States, Carolina Rice can reportedly trace its origins to a seventeenth-century sea captain who brought back from East Africa rice that he then cultivated in the coastal plantations of South Carolina. It's now grown mainly in Texas, Louisiana, Arkansas, and California.

+ **DELLA /** Raised and milled in small batches in the delta of East-Central Arkansas, the rice from this company produces delicious white and brown basmati, jasmine, and Arborio varieties. It's also a verified non-GMO product (one not genetically modified).

+ **POPCORN /** This Louisiana basmati hybrid, in white and brown long- and medium-grain forms, has a nuttiness and popcorn-like flavor that makes it one of my all-time favorites. Outside Louisiana it can be a bit tricky to find, but here are my go-to purveyors, all operating in the southwest reaches of the state: Cajun Country Rice, Campbell Farms, or Ellis Stansel's Gourmet Popcorn Rice.

+ **TEXMATI /** An aromatic rice originally developed near Galveston, Texmati is a hybrid of basmati and American long-grain rice, with a nutty flavor and fluffy consistency similar to popcorn rice. Its parent company, RiceSelect, is known for its commitment to organic, sustainable growing practices, with its WhiteStar product certified organic. Available in white, organic white, brown, light brown, and more.

+ **WILD PECAN /** Louisiana's Conrad Rice Mill near New Iberia's Bayou Teche is the oldest rice mill in America. Its Konriko Wild Pecan Rice is a long-grain variety that yields a nutty aroma and subtle pecan-like flavor (yet no pecans or wild rice are in it). It's gently milled to keep at least 85 percent of its bran layers to increase nutrition while decreasing cooking time to half that of brown rice.

+ For primo pasta, cook it about 2 minutes less than its package suggests for al dente; that firm texture will be perfect for continuing to cook (and hold its own) in a casserole.

+ Don't put pasta into the water until the water boils; otherwise you'll end up with a gooey mess. There should be about 4 quarts of water per 1 pound of pasta.

+ Salt the boiling water generously to season noodles as they cook. (It should taste like the sea.) Start with about 1 tablespoon and after cooking, see if that works for you; from there you'll know what to do in the future.

+ Adding oil will keep your pasta from sticking to your pan, but unfortunately, it also will keep your pasta from sticking to your sauce. Stir your pasta frequently during the first couple minutes of cooking and that should eliminate sticking issues. If using a lightweight stockpot, you may want to add just a touch of oil, since pasta will stick a bit more in pots that don't conduct heat evenly, like heavy-grade pots with a nonstick coating.

+ Don't cover your boiling pot of pasta; it will overflow.

+ Only run cold water over the pasta if planning to use the noodles later (and you want to stop the cooking process and retain its al dente texture). Ideally you should use the pasta immediately, skipping the cold rinse in order to keep the starch in place so it'll best absorb the forthcoming sauce.

+ Twelve-inch metal tongs are ideal for picking up cooked pasta and keeping it from slithering hither and yon. Better yet, cook pasta within a pot outfitted with a colander that can be removed without touching the pasta. The less you touch the pasta (and remove its sauce-magnet starchy coating), the better.

+ Pasta will freeze well if cooked to al dente texture and frozen in an airtight or vacuum-sealed bag. (A tiny straw works great for sucking out any excess air before zipping the bag fully closed.) To reheat, quickly plunge it into boiling water and within about a minute, it's back in action. Pasta that's been cooked to a soft texture before freezing will be even softer when reheated, so freezing might not be a good idea when it's easier just to cook a new and improved batch.

+ For my thoughts on no-boil noodles, see "Note," page 122.

DRIED PASTA	MINUTES TO PRECOOK FOR CASSEROLE*
Angel Hair	2 to 3
Elbow Macaroni	5
Fettuccine	11
Lasagna	8
Linguine	11
Penne/Ziti	10 to 12
Rigatoni	12
Rotini	7
Spaghetti	9
Vermicelli	5

* Suggested boiling times are about 2 minutes shy of al dente; the firmer texture keeps the pasta from getting too soft (read: mushy) while baking. Times may vary 1 to 2 minutes, depending on pasta type (i.e., whole wheat takes a minute or so longer to cook in general).

If anything defines a casserole in the South more than any other region of our great country, it's a casserole with grits (or, to a non-Southerner, polenta). Another distinctive Southern touch is adding cornbread to a dish (or, for a more Mexican touch, masa harina, a meal made from specially treated corn). Cornmeal-centric spoonbread is yet another cultural curiosity/delicacy, especially in the Deep South. But grits are what make us most famous, and differences between grits, polenta, and cornmeal relate to the corn type, grain size, and milling process.

Grits aren't a Southern invention; centuries ago, Native Americans made them from both dried corn and hominy. But it's the grits milled from coarsely ground white or yellow corn that have become the stuff of legend. We see them mostly in breakfast dishes, and paired with shrimp (Charleston style), or served with red-eye or tomato gravy (Tennessee style). Cheese grits are a delicious side dish to almost anything, especially with pork chops/sausage and catfish. Leftover grits can be made creamier with the addition of more milk, baked or fried as grit cakes (patties), or sliced into squares or triangles and grilled.

Historically, white corn grits, which have an earthier, more nuanced fragrance, were favored more in urban port areas (Charleston, New Orleans, Mobile), where European settlers resided and served the long-cooked creamy grits with refined seafood sauces. Yellow grits, with their more intense corn taste and rustic texture, were favored in the countryside, where yellow corn was plentiful (since it also fed farm animals). Country folk cooked them as porridge or fried them hoecake style, topping them with down-home sauces sometimes made with leftover coffee (red-eye gravy, anyone?). Nowadays, both are just a matter of taste. And color: Blue corn grits are increasingly popular. For those, I love the goods produced by the Homestead Gristmill near Waco, Texas (Homestead Gristmill.com).

+ **INSTANT /** Please don't eat this precooked, dehydrated, fine-grain mush unless you are trapped in your house and that's the only thing left to consume. They're the pinnacle of artificial flavor and texture and should not be confused with "quick" grits.

+ **QUICK /** These medium-grain grits, made from hominy, are a fine choice for grits needed in a hurry (about 5 minutes). Boil them in a pot with a tight lid. Add milk or half-and-half for a creamier consistency; add half water and half chicken broth for a more savory flavor. Add butter and cheese for more yumminess.

+ **STONE-GROUND /** These coarsely ground, heirloom-style grits, such as the ones made by Anson Mills (see "Lil' Dish," page 34) take more time to cook (an hour or longer) in a heavy-bottomed, tightly lidded saucepan over low heat. But they embody true-grit appeal, with a hearty flavor and toothsome texture that beautifully envelop cream, chicken broth, cheese, and fresh herbs to make them even more decadent.

+ **POLENTA /** This porridge of finely or coarsely ground yellow or white cornmeal, often boiled with chicken broth for a richer flavor, yields a creamier texture than most grits.

Creamy Stone-Ground Grits

○—— MAKES ABOUT 6 SERVINGS ——○

4 cups spring or filtered water (see Note)

2 tablespoons unsalted butter

¾ teaspoon ground sea or kosher salt

1 cup coarse stone-ground white grits

1 cup whole milk or half-and-half

¼ teaspoon ground black pepper

In a 3- to 4-quart heavy-bottomed saucepan, bring the water, 1 tablespoon of the butter, and the salt to a boil. Add the grits slowly, stirring constantly with a wooden spoon. Cover and reduce the heat to a simmer, stirring occasionally, until the water is absorbed and the grits are thickened, 12 to 15 minutes.

Add ½ cup of the milk and continue to simmer for 10 minutes, partially covered, stirring occasionally to prevent the grits sticking to the bottom of the pan. Stir in the remaining ½ cup milk and continue to simmer, partially covered, stirring occasionally, until all the liquid is absorbed and the grits are tender and thick, 40 minutes. Stir in the pepper and the remaining 1 tablespoon butter. Adjust the seasonings as desired before serving.

NOTE: Anson Mills (see "Lil' Dish," at right) suggests using spring or filtered water to ensure the softest texture without any "off" flavors.

Storage This can be made in advance and reheated with a bit more cream. Cooked, it will keep well tightly covered in the refrigerator for several days and it will freeze for up to 2 months (you'll want to defrost it overnight in the refrigerator and reheat it on a stovetop, adding a bit more milk or half-and-half to reenergize it). See "Just Chill" (page 41) for more tips.

◆ LIL' DISH ◆

ANSON MILLS—KEEPING IT REAL

Inspired to re-create the lost Southern dishes of his mother's childhood in Aiken, South Carolina, historic preservationist Glenn Roberts sold all his belongings in 1998 and purchased four native granite mills near Charleston. His aim was to grow and mill near-extinct varieties of heirloom corn, rice, and wheat. These ingredients, once staples of a pre–Civil War Southern regional cuisine, had vanished, taking with them the legacy of old-fashioned grits, cornbread, and biscuits. Roberts started by tracking down the elusive Carolina Gourdseed White corn, once used in grits, which he found growing wild in a bootlegger's field. One thing led to another, and today Anson Mills grows and mills more than a dozen varieties of heirloom corn, rice, wheat, buckwheat, oats, and farro. Order directly from AnsonMills.com.

One of the most highly coveted components of a casserole is its crust. That's why nearly everyone stealthily scoops up as much of it as they can when it's their turn at the dish (and woe betide the last soul to get there). That's why I often make two casseroles for a crowd, putting them out at the same time—just to ensure everyone gets a good-looking scoop or wedge. Consider these tip toppings and top tips.

✤ BAKING MIX / Southerners love Bisquick, and its taste isn't too far off the homespun mark. Use it for dumplings and regular or drop biscuits, and know that just as with cornbread, ingredients can be added for more flavor (I especially like adding rosemary to chicken pot pie dough). Their lighter version is a nice, healthful option.

✤ BISCUITS / Oh how I worship thee, Nathalie Dupree, and your Easy Cream Biscuits. (Try the recipe on page 36 and you'll see what I mean.) You can use the recipe in dough form—as one complete layer or as drop biscuits—but know that using this method will lend more of a lightly browned dumpling effect. You can, however, use cooked biscuit bottoms to line the bottom of a dish and the tops to top it; just make sure you cover the casserole top with foil so the biscuits won't get too brown. As for the canned variety, their texture can be comforting but their taste is a bit artificial. I do understand, however, how handy they can be when time's short. The larger canned biscuits can make quick and clever toppings for individual-size casseroles in ramekins.

✤ CORNBREAD / Use your favorite recipe (see mine on page 143) to mix and add as a layer atop the dish, or drop dollops of it atop the filling to make dumplings. Add green chiles, cilantro, or cheese to the dough to make it even yummier.

✤ CROISSANTS (CRESCENT-SHAPED DOUGH) / Like puff pastry, work with it very cold or you'll have a sticky mess. Try not to overhandle it to keep it as tender as possible; baby it and press at the seams only until just blended. Speaking of seams, Pillsbury now offers a seamless version, Recipe Creations. If you can find it, that will save you a little time.

✤ CRUMBLES AND SUCH / To give a casserole more crunch, consider using plain and buttered or flavored bread crumbs (Japanese panko gets the crispest); French-fried onion rings; corn, tortilla, or potato chips; crumbs from buttery crackers (think Ritz and Club); crumbled bacon; chopped toasted nuts; and, of course, cheese—which always makes people's eyes light up.

✤ MASHED POTATOES / Leftover homemade mashed potatoes (from russets and sweet potatoes) are ideal for topping a casserole like shepherd's pie or putting in a piping bag with a large tip to have them decoratively line a casserole dish (à la "Duchess" style). I prefer homemade or frozen mashed potatoes (adding cream cheese and chives to them) but flaked varieties will also work in a pinch.

✤ PHYLLO / Here's yet another multilayered beauty (but a little more fragile and temperamental than croissant dough). Fresh, unfrozen phyllo, which often can be found at Middle Eastern markets, is the primo choice, but mostly we're left with using the frozen variety. The main thing is not to let it defrost at room temperature: Moisture will accumulate too quickly and make the dough gummy and hard to separate. It's best to thaw it for 24 hours in the refrigerator. Since phyllo dries out quickly (within several minutes), it's "most important," as my mother would say, to keep it covered with a barely damp kitchen towel while working with it one sheet at a time.

+ **PIE CRUST (REFRIGERATED, FROZEN, SHELL) /** If you don't have the time or inclination to make your own crust, Pillsbury's Refrigerated Pie Crusts (two per package) are very good (and freeze well for up to 2 months, which is great when you only need one). For a bottom crust, prick the dough as much as possible (or use pie weights) and prebake a refrigerated one to a light golden brown for 10 to 12 minutes; a frozen/thawed or homemade one for 7 to 12 minutes. Pillsbury's frozen Pet-Ritz Pie Crust also has a nice texture and flavor, and is better than most others. Speaking of frozen, if that's all you have or want and need a topping for your dish, let two shells thaw, remove one from its tray, and use it to top the other, pressing it to seal decoratively. Create slits in the top to allow steam to vent.

+ **PUFF PASTRY /** With its light, airy crust, this offers one of the most elegant presentations and tastes. Like most refrigerated dough, it works best when cold (and if it's frozen, it will need about a day in the refrigerator to thaw). Even utensils and work surfaces (e.g., a silicone sheet) should be refrigerated beforehand. Hang on to dough scraps and think about using small cookie cutters to make decorative cutouts (leaves, hearts, etc.) to press on top. For ways to give a pastry crust shine and support, try a simple egg wash:

  + *For a yellow-golden, shiny pastry /* Brush the pastry with 1 egg yolk mixed with 1 tablespoon water or milk/cream.

  + *For a golden-brown, high-gloss pastry /* Brush the pastry with 1 egg white mixed with 1 tablespoon water or milk/cream.

NOTE: Use the egg-white wash on the bottom crust during prebaking. It will help create a seal to keep the filling from making the crust soggy.

Easy Cream Biscuits
MAKES 12-16 BISCUITS

Follow this recipe precisely and you'll be guaranteed heavenly light, creamy biscuits. It is adapted from *Southern Biscuits* by Nathalie Dupree and Cynthia Graubart. These fluffy lil' numbers create a pillowy base in Nathalie's exquisite brunch casserole (see page 115).

Melted butter for brushing the pan and biscuits

2¼ cups White Lily self-rising flour (see Note and "Lil' Dish," page 38)

1¼ cups cream

Adjust your oven rack to one of the top positions, setting the rack one shelf above the middle, but not so close to the top of the oven that the biscuits will bump into it as they rise.

Preheat the oven to 450°F.

For a soft exterior, select an 8- or 9-inch cake pan, pizza pan, or ovenproof skillet. The biscuits will nestle together snugly, helping them stay tender but rise while baking. Brush the pan with butter.

For a crisp overall exterior, select a baking sheet or large baking pan where the biscuits can be spaced wide apart, allowing air to circulate and create a crisp exterior. Brush the pan with butter.

In a large bowl, fork-sift or whisk 2 cups of the flour. Make a deep hollow in the center of the flour with the back of your hand. Pour 1 cup of the cream into the hollow and stir with a rubber spatula or large metal spoon, using broad circular strokes to quickly pull the flour into the cream. Mix just until the dry ingredients are moistened and the sticky dough begins to pull away from the sides of the bowl. If there is some flour remaining

[CONTINUED]

on the bottom and sides of the bowl, stir in 1 to 4 tablespoons of the remaining cream, just enough to incorporate the remaining flour into the shaggy, wettish dough. If the dough seems too wet, use more flour when shaping.

Lightly sprinkle a baking sheet or other clean surface with some of the remaining flour. Turn the dough out onto the board and sprinkle it lightly with flour. Flour your hands and then fold the dough over in half. Pat the dough into a round $\frac{1}{3}$ to $\frac{1}{2}$ inch thick, using a little additional flour if the dough is sticky. Fold the dough in half a second time. If the dough is still lumpy, pat and fold it a third time.

Pat the dough into a round $\frac{1}{2}$ inch thick for a normal biscuit, $\frac{3}{4}$ inch thick for a tall biscuit, and 1 inch thick for a giant biscuit. Brush off any visible flour from the top.

Dip a $2\frac{1}{2}$-inch biscuit cutter in flour and cut out the biscuits, starting at the outside edge and cutting very close together, being careful not to twist the cutter. Reflour the cutter after each biscuit. (The scraps may be combined to make additional biscuits, although these scraps make tougher biscuits.)

Using a metal spatula, move the cream biscuits to the pan or baking sheet. Place them with sides touching for a softer biscuit or spaced about 1 inch apart for a crispier exterior. Bake for 6 minutes, then rotate the pan so the front is now turned to the back. If the bottoms are browning too quickly, slide another baking pan underneath to add insulation. Continue baking for another 4 to 8 minutes, until they are lightly golden brown.

When the biscuits are done (within a total of 10 to 14 minutes), remove them from the oven and lightly brush the tops with butter. Turn the biscuits out upside down on a plate to cool slightly. Serve hot, right-side up.

NOTE: If there's no local source for White Lily and no time to order it, I'm so very sorry. But you can somewhat substitute it with one part all-purpose flour and one part cake flour (so for this recipe, use 1 cup plus 2 tablespoons all-purpose flour and 1 cup plus 2 tablespoons cake flour).

Storage

Biscuits will keep well in an airtight container for about 1 week in the refrigerator. They will freeze well for up to 2 months if you wrap them tightly in heavy-duty aluminum foil or freezer wrap and pack in freezer bags. Let biscuits defrost overnight in the refrigerator or use the microwave on the defrost setting.

LIL' DISH

WHITE LILY'S CULINARY CHARMS

We Southerners are blessed to have White Lily flour within easy reach of our local grocers' shelves, as it produces high-rising cloud-like biscuits, cakes, and pastries. Folks north of the Mason-Dixon Line will most likely have to order it online. But this is one flour you'll want to stock up on. Lighter than most, White Lily is milled from 100 percent pure, soft red winter wheat, whose low protein and gluten content produces the very best baking flour. Founded in 1883 in Knoxville, Tennessee, as the Knoxville Milling Company, White Lily has changed hands over the decades and is now made in Ohio (perish the thought!), but it still manages to maintain its superior quality. To order, visit OnlineStore.Smucker.com.

Some fifteen years ago, while dining at a friend's home in Birmingham, Alabama, we'd just enjoyed the most delicious Tex-Mex casserole—and I just had to have the recipe. I was shocked to learn that it came from *Cooking Light* magazine. (All that cheese and sour cream . . . *really?*) It hit me then that simply by making a few non-drastic but doable substitutions whenever possible, you could help a dish retain its flavor while trimming its fat and calories.

+ Cook with nonstick skillets and utensils.

+ Grease dishes with a nonstick vegetable spray.

+ Grill, broil, bake, or steam your food to avoid needing extra cooking fat.

+ Buy low-fat or nonfat dairy products (milk, cheese, yogurt). Substitute low-fat or nonfat cottage cheese for ricotta or use yogurt to replace or supplement recipes calling for sour cream, mayonnaise, cream cheese, buttermilk, heavy cream, and more (Chobani.com has an excellent conversion chart).

+ Substituting low-sodium chicken or beef broths is an easy way to cut back on your sodium intake. You're apt not to miss the salt, especially, if you amp up the dish's herbs. Besides, it's always easy to giveth salt, not taketh away.

+ Use herbs, spices, garlic and ginger, citrus juice/zest, flavored vinegars (rice-wine or balsamic), and low-sodium soy sauces to amp up the flavor and distract from missing fat or lower sodium.

+ Make lighter pasta sauces with a chunky-tomato marinara or add just enough olive oil, chicken broth, fat-free half-and-half, or light sour cream to create a sleek base for a touch of freshly grated, full-bodied Parmigiano-Reggiano or Parmesan cheese.

+ Reduce your intake of saturated fats (butter, lard) and use more monounsaturated (plant-based) fats such as olive, canola, and peanut oils and polyunsaturated fats, including safflower, corn, and sesame oils.

+ Peel away that flavorful (but fat-laden) chicken skin from bone-in portions, and resist the temptations of dark meat. You can do it. You are stronger than you think. More healthful boneless, skinless chicken breasts can easily be cubed or shredded or sliced nicely into whatever you're cooking.

+ Give ground chicken and turkey a try instead of ground beef; they both have about half the calories. The same reasoning stands for using preseasoned turkey or chicken sausage instead of Italian beef/pork.

+ Maneuver out of a chicken- or beef-eating rut by including more pork, seafood, vegetables, and soy in your diet. Salmon, for instance, is a heart-healthy food, and shrimp is full of protein and zinc. Tofu, low in fat and high in calcium and vegetable protein, can be beautifully seared and cooked to taste, well, just like chicken.

+ Cut back on red meat. Start by using less of it than usual, replacing some of it with hefty bits of zucchini or mushrooms to bulk up your dish without losing the beefy flavor.

+ Serve a salad and a light vinaigrette with your casserole; that'll reduce the urge to go get main-dish seconds.

+ Skip the toasted, buttered bread side offering.

+ Work more whole grains (especially pastas) and vegetables (black beans, sweet potatoes, and spinach) into your dishes.

+ Give yourself smaller portions on smaller plates and eat until you're satisfied, not full.

Slow cooking opens up another world of casserole possibilities—and time, energy, and money savings. There are a number of good books and online sources, but in general, here's what to know:

+ Crockery cookers and slow cookers are used interchangeably, though technically they're not the same; the former heat from the sides and bottom, the latter only from the bottom. (I'm of the camp that calls them all slow cookers, so indulge me.) Also, why do I refer to one as a "crockery cooker" when everybody and her cousin calls it a Crock-Pot? Well, it's just like goin' to get soft drinks is "goin' to get Cokes" in the South. Crock-Pot is actually a registered trademark for the product made by Rival, and obviously they don't want other companies horning in on the branding they've worked on since 1970.

+ Crockery cookers have the simplest of settings: "High," for continuous heat at about 300°F, and "Low," for about 200°F. Increasingly they feature programmable timers and high-tech digital bells and whistles. These are especially great for tenderizing pot roasts and less-expensive cuts of meat that would usually require monitoring for a long time over low heat (that also would heat up your home). Having a tightly sealed, well-insulated pot that manages all that for you—often while you sleep—is a definite plus, especially if it's dishwasher-safe.

+ Slow cookers differ from electric crockery cookers in that they use heating elements at the bottom (as hot plates) and have more temperature-degree setting options. (My family always used them to cook briskets and such.) Because the heating element does not surround the pot, scorching food can be a problem unless you keep it stocked with liquid.

+ Round pots are ideal for small kitchens and small families, since they need less counter space than their oval brethren and are great for cooking smaller casseroles, roasts, and stews. Those oval ones are perfect for cooking bigger casseroles, turkeys, a couple of whole chickens, or larger cuts of meat—perfect for large families or parties.

+ Pots shouldn't be filled more than three-quarters full to allow for heat to evenly circulate around the food.

+ Clear glass lids keep you from being tempted to lift the top to check in on your dish. Each time that you do, you tack on about 5 minutes of cooking time.

+ To adapt an oven-cooked casserole for use in a slow cooker, look for similar ones in cookbooks or online. You'll see that most liquids need to be reduced by about 25 percent, since evaporation isn't a concern for slow cooking (juices collected on the lid double as baster).

+ Automatic timers are great, but don't allow your food to sit in the pot for more than 2 hours before cooking kicks in. If you'll be cutting it close, put your food in the pot very cold.

+ Slow cookers use about the same energy as a 75-watt bulb—much less than an oven. They also won't heat your kitchen—a bonus during the South's summer swelter.

Slow-cooker time frames:

FOOD	HIGH	LOW
Casseroles	2 to 4 hours	4 to 9 hours
Chicken	3 to 4 hours	7 to 10 hours
Meat loaf	3 to 4 hours	8 to 10 hours
Pot roast	4 to 5 hours	8 to 10 hours

Anything can be frozen and reheated. Now whether you *like* what you see and taste is something else altogether. (My culinarily hapless mother once stuck a leftover boiled crab in our freezer door, and when I opened it, the silly thing came flying at me. To say I shrieked is an understatement.) Truth is, freezing precooked casseroles with potatoes, pasta, or rice isn't a good idea; moisture loss makes them mushy. It's best to prepare them for baking and then freeze. But I know you'll do what you want to do and I'm not here to judge—just offer these tips:

THE BASICS

+ Keep your freezer at 0°F; the more you put in it, the more you'll need to increase its cooling power. Allow enough room around each frozen packet to keep good airflow/circulation. Don't let it get more than 75 percent full.

+ Unbaked casseroles freeze best, but you can undercook your dish by about half its normal baking time to eliminate some of the total time. If it's to be covered with cheese, use only about half as much; just before baking, add the final portion to give it the freshest look and texture. Add anything meant to be crispy (crackers, fried onions) just before baking.

+ Use a fine-point indelible marker to write the casserole's name, preparation date, number of servings, reheating instructions, and use-by date on a large peel-and-stick freezer label or piece(s) of freezer tape.

+ Frozen casseroles are best eaten within 2 or 3 months. After that, they're prone to freezer burn, which occurs when dehydration allows more air to get in and damages the food's texture and flavor.

+ Freezing leftovers (unless done the day the casserole was cooked) is not advised; an "off" flavor could develop.

+ Keep frozen food layers no more than 2 inches deep in order for them to freeze quickly; this helps reduce the formation of ice crystals, which compromise a dish's flavor.

+ Tomato-based casseroles like lasagna don't fare well cooked in aluminum pans; it causes acid to leach into the metal, creating a tinnish flavor. It's best to heavily grease or coat a nonaluminum pan with nonstick cooking spray, line it with parchment paper, and then add the casserole ingredients before baking or freezing.

+ Out of sight, out of mind. That's what happens when you put a bunch of stuff in the freezer and ultimately end up throwing it out because you simply forgot it was there. Keep a list of what's in the freezer, maybe next to where you keep a running grocery list (perhaps behind a pantry door).

REHEATING SMARTS

+ Thaw a frozen casserole in the refrigerator at least 8 hours or overnight before cooking; this will allow for more even reheating.

+ When running short on time, if your frozen casserole is in (or can be put in) a microwave-safe dish before baking, defrost it following your microwave's instructions (usually 7 to 10 minutes per 1 pound of food on the lowest cook setting) before baking. However, I don't advise actually cooking the dish in the microwave because often the outside will appear nice and bubbly, leading you to believe it's cooked through. In reality, the interior may be frozen solid while the outside can promptly remove the top layer of your lips.

+ Listen up, people: Freezing food does not kill bacteria. So do not, under any circumstances, allow anything frozen to thaw at room temperature or warmer (like outside on a porch). Doing so will encourage a rapid spread of bacteria. It's best to let a casserole thaw in the refrigerator overnight. You also can defrost it in the microwave, but because it will be warm when defrosted you'll need to cook it immediately to stop bacterial growth. Another option is to put the food in a waterproof container and submerge it in cold (not hot or warm) water, changing the water every 30 minutes to keep it cold until thawing is complete (usually 2 or 3 hours for a 3- to 4-pound casserole).

+ Reheat thawed, cooked dishes at 350°F, covered, until the center of the casserole reaches 165°F, or the casserole is thoroughly heated (usually the same as the original cooking time). Reducing the temperature helps keep the dish from losing too much moisture or browning too much, but it will take longer to cook.

+ If cooking from frozen, plan on at least 50 percent more cooking time, sometimes double, depending on the depth of the dish.

+ Make sure the center of the food reaches an internal temperature of 165°F and its edges are bubbly.

+ Very cold glass baking dishes can break if put into a preheated oven; check to ensure they are "oven-safe."

+ For more on food preservation, head online to the National Center for Home Food Preservation (nchfp.uga.edu), a collaborative project of The University of Georgia and Alabama A&M, with input from a variety of home economists and other universities.

TAKE FIVE: EASY FREEZING

1 Line the baking pan with heavy-duty aluminum foil, letting the foil hang over each side, enough so that it can later fold over the casserole. (Temporarily fold the foil under the dish while you're creating the casserole.) This way, you can remove it from the pan and use the pan again before you reheat the casserole.

2 Press a sheet of plastic wrap or wax paper across the top of the prepared casserole (to help prevent water crystals from forming) and wrap the dish tightly with the surrounding foil. Add another layer of foil if desired. Freeze the casserole in the dish.

3 Lift the foil-wrapped frozen casserole from the dish and either:

  + Place it in a large zip-top freezer or vacuum-sealed bag.

  + Cover it with freezer paper (available at most supermarkets) and seal with freezer tape.

  + Place it in an appropriately sized, airtight freezer container.

4 Label the tightly covered casserole with at least the recipe's name and preparation date. The more information noted, however, the better. (See "The Basics," page 41.)

5 Before cooking, remove it from its mummy wrapping and place it back in the very dish in which it was first assembled.

Follow these tips to give your casserole sprightlier taste:

+ Embolden its flavor with herbs, fresh or dried.

+ For style and flavor: Strategically place whole flat-leaf parsley or cilantro leaves or toss on green onions sliced on the bias or, do as the French do: create an herb *chiffonade* (pronounced shihf-uh-NAHD or shihf-un-NAYD) by cutting a leafy herb (basil, sage, mint) or vegetable (spinach or lettuce) into super-thin and elegant ribbon-like strips. To do this, wash the leaves and remove any extending stems. Stack 7 or 8 leaves, from largest on the outside to smallest on the inside. Roll them tightly lengthwise, stems facing down, cigar style. Aim a chef's knife at a 60-degree angle to carefully cut slices $\frac{1}{16}$ to $\frac{1}{8}$ inch thick. Fluff the slices with your fingers before sprinkling them atop your dish. **NOTE:** You can do this with spinach and kale, but you'll get more nutrient and color impact than a flavor one.

+ Drain and rinse canned vegetables very well to remove any metallic-tasting brine.

+ Add a squeeze or two of fresh lemon, lime, or orange juice or toss in some freshly grated zest.

+ Use freshly grated aged Parmesan cheese instead of the milder pregrated variety.

+ Since most dried herbs have a more concentrated flavor than fresh, a good rule of thumb is to know that 1 teaspoon of dried herbs equals 1 tablespoon of fresh (a one-to-three ratio). To get the best flavor out of the dried variety, rub it gently between your thumb and forefinger before adding to your dish.

+ Keep your favorite spice blend handy to spike whatever you're cooking. Three of my favorites are Emeril's Essence, Stubb's Rosemary-Ginger Rub, and McCormick Italian Seasoning Herb Grinder.

+ Use freshly pressed garlic instead of garlic powder.

+ Add a pinch of cayenne pepper or dash of hot sauce.

+ Give it more oniony flavor with green onions or caramelized sweet onions.

+ Serve salsa, spiced fruit chutney, or chowchow (vegetable relish) to complement your dish.

+ Use real butter instead of margarine, and cream instead of milk. (*Yes*, I know this goes against what I advise in the "Do the Lighten Up" section, but sometimes you can—and frankly must—live a little. As Oscar Wilde said, "Everything in moderation, including moderation.")

+ Add a few drops of malt vinegar or Worcestershire sauce for oomph.

+ Grind some sea salt (including flavored ones) and peppercorns (including mixed ones) instead of using iodized salt and standard pepper. Speaking of the latter, my food-writing muse, Eugene Walter of Mobile, referred to basic pepper as "dead pepper," and in restaurants would make a waiter or dining companion hide it from sight.

+ Add a splash of sherry or wine to the sauce while sautéing seafood, chicken, or vegetables.

+ Cook rice in chicken or beef broth (depending on what it'll be paired with) and grits in cream and/or chicken broth instead of water.

+ Sprinkle on crisp, crumbled bacon . . . sweet, sweet bacon . . .

+ Top your casserole with some crunch: Think French-fried onion rings, crumbled corn or crushed tortilla chips, buttery crackers (à la Ritz or Club), buttery bread crumbs, and toasted chopped pecans.

+ For sweet casseroles, such as pies, cobblers, and trifles, top with granulated or powdered sugar, a streusel blend, shaved chocolate, sliced or whole fruit, sprigs of fresh mint, or whipped cream spiked with a bit of sugar and perhaps a liqueur.

A TOAST TO NUTS

To bring out the fullest flavor of whatever nut you're featuring in your dish, spread a layer of them on a rimmed baking sheet and bake at 350°F for 5 to 7 minutes, shaking the pan and/or turning them with a spatula about halfway through the toasting time. When you start smelling them, they're usually ready. Let them cool before handling.

To put a proverbial feather in your casserole's cap (and yours), consider these decorative and edible toppings:

Boiled egg slices: To kick it old school

Cheese: Just a sprinkling, added 5 minutes before the casserole leaves the oven, will make the prettiest impression

Dried herbs: Use a delicate hand

Edible flowers: For sweet casseroles

Fresh fruit: Whole or sliced, for sweet casseroles

Fresh herbs: Whole, chopped, or thinly sliced parsley, chives, cilantro, basil, rosemary, thyme, oregano

Green onions: Thinly sliced or cut on the bias

Lettuce: Shredded

Olives: Kalamata, green, or black; sliced

Peppers: Rings of small green, red, and/or yellow bell peppers; one or more whole jalapeños placed decoratively at the center or sliced and placed strategically near sour cream dollops

Seasonings: Paprika, Southwest, or Cajun (but watch the salt in the latter two)

Sour cream: A dollop or more

Streusel: For sweet casseroles

Tomatoes: Diced or as wedges

Casseroles are usually a meal in one, but you really ought to have a little something green (or yellow or orange) to go with a starchy, meaty main dish. (Especially so you don't go back for seconds on that heavy stuff—unless you're not watching your figure, and then I envy you.) Consider a salad with a light vinaigrette that doesn't compete with your casserole's flavor, or maybe a good ol' American salad with a creamy, always-right ranch dressing. Or maybe coleslaw.

Steamed, lightly seasoned broccoli, green beans, zucchini, squash, and/or carrots (more on the chunky side so as not to be chased around the plate) also make nice accompaniments. So does fresh fruit alongside breakfast casseroles. If company's coming, offer a light dessert—a fruity sorbet or ice cream, perhaps—since the meal will be a heavy one and there likely won't be room for anything other than a creamy-cool treat.

When it comes to preventing foodborne illnesses, the biggest culprits are casseroles cooked for crowds. You can do your best to be "pot-lucky."

Perishable food can sometimes be left at room temperature too long. Or someone's food may have been cooked and not allowed to cool properly before being only slightly reheated. Or maybe someone defrosted her hamburger meat on a kitchen counter for, oh, say, twelve hours. Or another person brought the spoon they used to handle their casserole's chicken when it was raw—but it hasn't been washed and is now stuck in the cooked dish. You just don't know. But you *can* do your own part in keeping others safe. These straightforward food-safety rules can prevent illness:

✢ Wash hands, cutting boards, and utensils in hot soapy water after cutting raw meat, poultry, or fish and before handling other foods. Use a plastic cutting board instead of a wooden one, where bacteria can hide in cracks and deep scratches.

✢ Always thaw food in the refrigerator (see page 41).

✢ Cook meats to their minimum internal temperatures, checking doneness with a thermometer. See page 23 for a helpful chart.

✢ Once cooked, keep your casserole at 140°F degrees or hotter by keeping it in a chafing dish (see page 126), crockery cooker, or other warming appliance.

✢ If not serving your cooked casserole immediately, refrigerate it within 1 hour (sooner if your kitchen is hot). To allow excess moisture from steam to escape from a still-warm casserole (where bacteria can begin to breed), keep it uncovered on the top shelf of the refrigerator until cold, then cover.

✢ Don't fill your storage containers too full: Two inches deep is enough to allow for a quick cool-down before refrigerating or freezing.

✢ Make sure your refrigerator is set no higher than 40°F and that your freezer is set at 0°F. Buy temperature gauges to monitor accuracy.

✢ Keep cold foods cold (40°F or below).

✢ A just-cooked casserole straight from the oven will stay hot (above 140°F) en route to your event if it's well insulated. Use a few layers of aluminum foil, followed by newspapers and a towel. (And, if possible, transport it in a stylishly clever container.) Serve the casserole as soon as you arrive to the event or return it to the oven to get it back to the desired temperature.

✢ After serving your casserole, refrigerate it within 2 hours; sooner if possible. If it's been left out more than 2 hours, toss it. Seriously. Don't let someone talk you into keeping it "cause that's what preservatives are for."

✢ Rapidly reheat leftovers to a center temperature of at least 165°F to kill any bacteria that may have developed on the food while refrigerated.

✢ Don't refrigerate and reheat your food more than once.

✢ For more on freezing casseroles, see "Just Chill," page 41.

✣ Read a recipe all the way through before attempting to make it. That way you'll know what ingredients you'll need and can avoid technical missteps.

✣ The French call it *mise en place*; I call it having everything in place before setting out to make a recipe. Before shopping, check your pantry and refrigerator to save yourself from buying things you may not need (seasonings, for instance). Chop everything and have it ready to go and you'll save yourself some stress.

✣ Not sure if your casserole will fit a dish? Choose the larger of your options. No one will really care what it's in. But if the casserole bubbles over, spilling into your oven and creating a mess, *you'll* care what dish it is in. By that time, it will be quite the kerfuffle to divide it into two dishes.

✣ Keep a baking sheet under your casserole in the oven, especially if your dish is pretty close to full (or might spill over). This also helps you avoid accidentally touching the food with your oven mitts.

✣ Want to know the capacity of an unmarked casserole dish? Pour into it 1 quart of water at a time until you know about how many quarts it'll hold. Use an indelible marker on the underside of the dish to help you remember; also write your last name to help claim it after a potluck.

✣ Don't trust those plastic spice caps with sifter holes; always pour what you need into your hand or in a small bowl, or measure it out with spoon. In one case, my ¼ teaspoon dried red pepper flakes accidentally became ¼ cup when the cap fell off. Oy.

✣ If cooking immediately with ingredients still warm from being just cooked, your casserole will take less time to bake than had it been assembled and refrigerated in advance.

✣ The more food you cram in the oven to get cooked, the longer it'll take to get everything cooked evenly.

✣ Casseroles that bake in deeper pans than called for should bake for at least 25 minutes longer; the same reasoning goes for shallower dishes (think 25 minutes less).

✣ It's best to cook a casserole covered with aluminum foil until the last 10 minutes or so of baking. It's done when the edges are bubbling with vigor. Sometimes you may want the top to be more of a golden brown, so use the broiler to obtain that effect (but watch it closely so that you don't burn the thing).

✣ Casseroles should "rest" 7 to 10 minutes before serving to allow the flavors and texture to coalesce. Just don't let them rest for more than 2 hours at room temperature; you may think you're being a gracious host, but the result will be a flavor and food-safety buzzkill later.

✣ Don't put a hot dish directly on a surface without first placing a hot pad or trivet underneath.

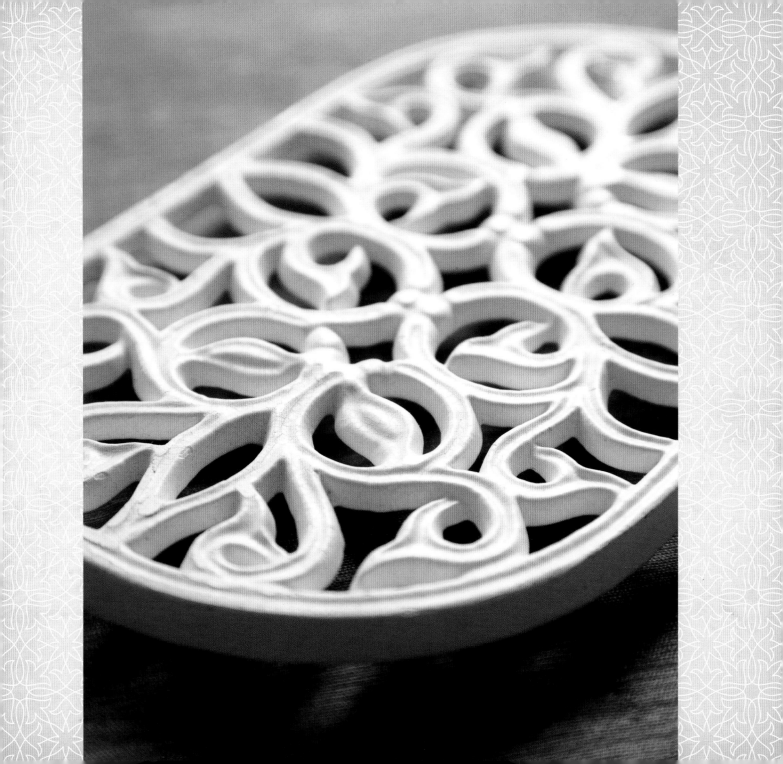

CHAPTER 02

Easy Eats

Bless the food that's really good when time's really short.
May I present to you the banquet chapter of the simplest-to-make,
easiest-to-please comfort food, perfect for eating at home or
taking to a social occasion. You've got your choice of spaghetti,
dumplings, cornbread, rice, grits, chicken, beef, sausage,
crawfish, shrimp, and more, all dolled up with few ingredients
and lots of flavor.

Jambalaya Ya-Ya

SERVES 4

To the early Greeks, *yaya* meant "woman"; now its meaning has morphed into "wise older woman" or "grandmother." Southern *ya-yas* are sisterhoods of wise women who've been there and done that, and now relish the good life. As for pretension, they're just plain over it. That pretty much sums up this Cajun dish, which is often served with hot sauce—and attitude—on the side.

2 TO 3 TABLESPOONS VEGETABLE OIL

8 TO 12 OUNCES SMOKED ANDOUILLE OR OTHER SAUSAGE, SLICED

1 CUP CHOPPED ONION

¾ CUP CHOPPED CELERY

2 GARLIC CLOVES, MINCED

ONE 14.5-OUNCE CAN DICED TOMATOES WITH GREEN CHILES, WITH THEIR JUICES

1½ CUPS UNCOOKED LONG-GRAIN RICE

1 TABLESPOON FRESH OR 1 TEASPOON DRIED OREGANO

½ TEASPOON CAJUN SEASONING

¼ TEASPOON GROUND BLACK PEPPER

2½ CUPS CHICKEN BROTH

1 POUND MEDIUM (41/50 COUNT) SHRIMP, PEELED AND DEVEINED (SEE NOTE)

1½ CUPS SLICED FRESH OKRA OR ONE 10-OUNCE BAG FROZEN, THAWED AND DRAINED

GARNISH: SLICED GREEN ONIONS

1 Preheat the oven to 350°F.

2 In a Dutch oven, heat two tablespoons of the vegetable oil over medium heat and add the sausage. Cook, stirring occasionally, until the sausage is browned, 7 to 10 minutes. Remove the sausage to a medium bowl and set aside.

3 If less than 1 tablespoon of drippings remain in the Dutch oven, add the remaining 1 tablespoon oil (some sausages will leave more drippings than others). Add the onion, celery, and garlic and cook until tender, 5 to 7 minutes. Pour the diced tomatoes and their juices into the pan. Stir in the rice, oregano, Cajun seasoning, and black pepper.

4 Stir the broth into the pan along with the reserved sausage. Cover and bake for about 30 minutes, or until the rice is cooked. Uncover and gently fold in the shrimp (so the rice completely covers it) and okra. Re-cover the dish and cook for 10 to 12 minutes more, or until the rice is tender. Let stand covered for about 10 minutes before serving. Garnish each serving with green onions.

[CONTINUED]

NOTE: Instead of shrimp, consider using an equal amount of crawfish tails (with liquid from the package) or 1½ to 2 cups chopped cooked chicken or turkey.

Storage

Like gumbo, this tastes even better the day after you cook it (and tightly covered, it will refrigerate well for 2 days more), so it's a great make-ahead dish. If necessary, add more chicken broth to moisten the mixture before covering and reheating it over low heat, for 30 minutes, stirring occasionally and gently, until hot. Despite there being rice in this dish, it freezes OK (tightly covered for up to 1 month) because the acid in the tomatoes helps keep the long-grain rice stout. When reheating from frozen, place it (broken up in chunks if need be) in a Dutch oven with a few tablespoons of oil and let it thaw slowly, stirring occasionally, over very low heat until the mixture is heated thoroughly, adding chicken broth to moisten it as desired. See "Just Chill" (page 41) for more tips.

ANDOUILLE FOR DUMMIES

Many think of andouille pork sausage as hot and spicy. And sometimes it is—when made by a company, say, in Idaho. True andouille isn't hot. It's heavily smoked, often over pecan wood, which results in a deep, earthy, garlicky flavor and hefty texture that can't easily be replicated (or even explained). LaPlace, Louisiana, is the "Andouille Capital of the World," with family businesses Bailey's Sausage and Jacob's Sausage making the good stuff for more than one hundred years. By the way, the word *andouille* is French for "idiot." Keep that in your cap for when you want to fuss at a busybody in your kitchen.

Sissy's Spicy Shrimp & Cheese Grits

SERVES 8

As an impressionable Mississippi lass who wanted to absorb (literally and figuratively) everything I could about cooking, one of the kitchens in which I was most in awe was that of Sissy Eidt, mother of my friend Margaret. Sissy was constantly making casseroles, not only for her family, but also for others in need of edible TLC. And man, could she cook. This dish is a particular favorite. It's adapted from *Ladies' Legacies in Natchez*, a cookbook she co-wrote with her cousin Mary Eidt. This includes shrimp and crumbled bacon, which takes it over the top and on into heaven.

3 CUPS CHICKEN BROTH

1 CUP HALF-AND-HALF

1½ CUPS QUICK-COOKING GRITS (SEE PAGE 32)

1½ CUPS SHREDDED SHARP CHEDDAR CHEESE

ONE 10-OUNCE CAN ORIGINAL (MEDIUM SPICED) OR MILD DICED TOMATOES WITH GREEN CHILES (SUCH AS RO*TEL), DRAINED

1 TABLESPOON VEGETABLE OIL OR OLIVE OIL

1 GARLIC CLOVE, MINCED

1 TO 1½ POUNDS MEDIUM (41/50 COUNT) SHRIMP, PEELED AND DEVEINED

1 TEASPOON CAJUN SEASONING (SEE NOTE)

GARNISHES: CRISP AND CRUMBLED BACON, SLICED GREEN ONIONS

HOT SAUCE FOR SERVING (OPTIONAL)

1 Preheat the oven to 350°F.

2 In a medium heavy-bottom saucepan, bring the broth and half-and-half to a boil. Gradually stir in the grits. Reduce the heat to low and cover, stirring occasionally, for 8 to 10 minutes or until the grits are tender. Add the cheese and stir until melted. Remove from the heat, stir in the tomatoes, and set aside.

3 In a large skillet, heat the vegetable oil over medium-low heat. Add the garlic and sauté for about 2 minutes, until tender. Increase the heat to medium and add the shrimp and Cajun seasoning, stirring constantly until the shrimp are coated with seasoning yet not cooked through, about 1 minute.

4 Pour the grits into a lightly greased 2½-quart casserole dish. Fold in the shrimp, ensuring the grits cover them (to keep them tender while baking).

[CONTINUED]

5 Cover and bake for about 40 minutes, or until the casserole is set and the edges are golden. Garnish with the bacon and green onions, and serve with hot sauce on the side, if desired.

NOTE: Unless your Cajun seasoning is a lower-sodium version, you may want to use low-sodium chicken broth and adjust the salt content afterward.

Storage

The grits can be made up to 6 hours ahead and kept tightly covered and refrigerated until you're ready to cook the shrimp mixture and assemble the casserole. To revive the creamy texture, reheat the grits in a medium heavy-bottom saucepan, adding extra chicken broth or half-and-half if necessary. Cooked and tightly covered, the finished casserole will keep well in the refrigerator for up to 2 days. To freeze a cooked casserole (which should be done the day you cook it or the shrimp will have an "off" flavor), don't add the bacon or green onions. Mix the shrimp so that they're covered by the grits and freeze in an airtight container for up to 1 month. Defrost in the refrigerator overnight. See "Just Chill" (page 41) for more tips.

LIL' DISH

RO*TEL IT LIKE IT IS

Ro*Tel, a spiced tomato recipe, hails from a Texas Rio Grande Valley family. The year was 1943, and Carl Roettele was inspired to blend the richness of fresh tomatoes with the zestiness of green chile peppers. He and his wife opened a small canning plant in Elsa, at the very southern tip of the state. It wasn't until the 1960s, though, when Lyndon Baines Johnson moved into the White House, that he and other Texans began singing its praises, and the canned product rose as a nationally known Lone Star star.

Crawfish Fettuccine

This deluxe, quick-cooking seafood casserole is hugely popular
along the Gulf Coast. Double this for a big crowd and watch it go.

1 POUND DRIED FETTUCCINE OR LINGUINE, BROKEN IN HALF

⅓ CUP BUTTER

1 CUP DICED ONION

½ CUP DICED GREEN BELL PEPPER

⅓ CUP DICED CELERY

1 GARLIC CLOVE, MINCED

¼ CUP ALL-PURPOSE FLOUR

¾ CUP HALF-AND-HALF

1 POUND VELVEETA QUESO BLANCO OR OTHER PROCESSED CHEESE, CUBED (SEE NOTES)

1 POUND PEELED CRAWFISH TAILS, LIQUID RESERVED (SEE NOTES)

2 TABLESPOONS MINCED FRESH OR 2 TEASPOONS DRIED PARSLEY

½ TO 1 TEASPOON REDUCED-SODIUM CAJUN SEASONING (SEE NOTES)

PINCH OF CAYENNE PEPPER (OPTIONAL)

¼ CUP GRATED PARMESAN CHEESE

GARNISH: MINCED FRESH OR DRIED PARSLEY OR SLICED GREEN ONIONS (OPTIONAL)

1 Preheat the oven to 350°F.

2 Lightly grease a 13-by-9-inch or 3-quart casserole dish and set aside.

3 Cook the pasta in boiling water. Two minutes before its suggested cooking time, check to see if it's al dente (see "Use Your Noodle," page 31). If so, drain the pasta (but don't rinse it with water) and add it to a large bowl.

4 In a Dutch oven over medium heat, melt the butter. Add the onion, bell pepper, celery, and garlic and cook until tender, about 5 minutes. Add the flour and stir frequently for 2 to 3 minutes. Add the half-and-half and Velveeta and cook until the cheese is melted, stirring occasionally, 7 to 10 minutes. Add the crawfish tails with their liquid, parsley, Cajun seasoning, and cayenne (if using). Reduce the heat to low and simmer for 20 minutes.

5 Pour the crawfish sauce over the pasta and stir gently to combine. Spread it evenly into the prepared dish and top with the Parmesan. Bake for 25 to 30 minutes, or until the casserole is bubbly and the cheese is golden. Garnish with parsley and green onions, if desired, before serving.

NOTES: Velveeta's new queso blanco, a white processed cheese, lends a much nicer color to this dish.

Substitute 1 pound medium (41/50 count), peeled, uncooked shrimp if you can't find or don't want to use crawfish.

Since many Cajun seasonings can be a bit too salty, using a low-sodium version gives you the flavor while letting you adjust the salt level to your liking.

Storage

This can be made up to 8 hours before cooking (just don't add the garnish until after baking). Cooked and tightly covered, it will keep well in the refrigerator for up to 2 days and frozen for up to 3 months. See "Just Chill" (page 41) for more tips.

LIL' DISH

CRAWFISH: THE REAL DEAL

It can be tempting, I know. When buying crawfish, one price is often too good to be true. The package looks similar—the label even has a Cajun name—but if you look closely, you'll see it's imported from China. And because of the low production costs there, the "dumping" of below–market value (and often less tasty and healthy) crawfish has dealt Louisiana and Atchafalaya Basin crawfish farmers a tremendous blow. Buy local if at all possible: You'll not only be supporting a cherished Southern foodway, but also helping a fishing family do everything it can to stay in the game. (See Sources, page 167.)

Skillet Catfish-Pecan Bake

SERVES 4

Looking (and tasting) lovely nestled in cast iron, this recipe comes from one of my favorite Mississippi catfish vendors, Delta Pride. The Indianola-based company is actually a cooperative of some 115 members, who farm nearly 60,000 acres of catfish in the Mississippi Delta. As with Louisiana crawfish, I'm particular about my catfish, and hope to find either Mississippi-, Alabama-, Louisiana-, or Arkansas-raised catfish on the menu wherever I travel and dine. The subtle sweet flavor of Southern farm-raised catfish is unmistakable.

1½ POUNDS SOUTHERN FARM-RAISED CATFISH FILLETS, CUT ON THE DIAGONAL IN 2-INCH PIECES, RINSED AND WELL DRIED

2 TEASPOONS CAJUN SEASONING

3 TABLESPOONS OLIVE OIL OR PEANUT OIL

½ CUP CHOPPED CELERY

½ CUP CHOPPED GREEN OR RED BELL PEPPER

¼ CUP CHOPPED WHITE OR SWEET ONION

¼ CUP CHOPPED GREEN ONIONS

ONE 10.75-OUNCE CAN CREAM OF MUSHROOM SOUP

⅔ CUP HALF-AND-HALF

¼ CUP DRY SHERRY

2 TABLESPOONS FRESH LEMON JUICE

4 CUPS COOKED WILD RICE BLEND (STORE-BOUGHT OR SEE PAGE 103)

¼ CUP TOASTED PECAN PIECES (SEE PAGE 45)

½ TO 1 CUP GRATED SHARP CHEDDAR OR COLBY CHEESE

GARNISHES: SLICED GREEN ONIONS, TOASTED PECANS

1 Preheat the oven to 350°F.

2 In a medium bowl, evenly coat the catfish pieces with the Cajun seasoning.

3 In a large skillet, heat 1½ tablespoons of the olive oil over medium-low heat. When the oil is hot, about 1 minute, add the catfish pieces and sauté for 1 to 2 minutes per side, until they are light golden brown. Remove the catfish to a plate, cover with aluminum foil, and set aside.

4 Add the remaining 1½ tablespoons oil to the pan and, when hot, add the celery, bell pepper, and white and green onions and cook, stirring frequently, until tender, 5 to 7 minutes. Add the soup, half-and-half, sherry, and lemon juice; stir well to combine. Simmer 2 to 3 minutes, or until bubbly. Taste and adjust the seasonings.

5 Add the wild rice to a 13- to 15-inch cast-iron skillet (at least 2¼ inches deep) or 10- to 12-inch cast-iron skillet (at least 3 inches deep). Top with the catfish mixture, pecans, and cheese. Cover with a lid or foil.

6 Bake for 25 minutes; uncover and cook for 5 minutes more, or until the cheese is melted and the sauce is bubbly. Serve garnished with green onion and pecans.

Storage

Tightly covered, this will keep well in the refrigerator for 1 day. I wouldn't recommend freezing it because of the delicate texture of the fish that will already be soft in the cooking sauce. It will freeze well enough in an airtight container for up to 1 month if you mix it so that the rice covers the cooked fish by about 1 inch. Cook it directly from frozen (adding more cheese near the end of baking). See "Just Chill" (page 41) for more tips.

See "Just Chill" (page 41) for more tips.

LIL' DISH

LODGE: IRONCLAD SUCCESS

Cast iron has long been part and parcel of Southern cooking—primarily for frying chicken and fish or making crispy cornbread. And one Southern family has spent four generations perfecting it. Lodge Cast Iron, founded by Joseph Lodge in 1896, is the oldest manufacturer of cast-iron cookware in the country. The company's beloved Dutch ovens, casseroles, and skillets are still made to strict standards by artisans in the tiny town of South Pittsburg, Tennessee, near the Cumberland Plateau of the Appalachian Mountains. A privately held metal formula, precision molds, and exacting mold-wall thickness produce cookware that heats and retains heat more evenly than stainless and aluminum. (And now that it's available pre-seasoned, who can resist?)

Classic Tetrazzini

Because my family loves asparagus, and it's plentiful and cheap in the spring, we often added it to our Tetrazzini (and also didn't use canned soup for it). That's a tradition I still follow, which gives it a prettier, fresher-tasting advantage over other Tetrazzinis. Be sure not to rinse your hot, cooked pasta—the starch that clings to it will help your sauce better adhere to it.

---

12 OUNCES DRIED VERMICELLI OR THIN SPAGHETTI, BROKEN IN HALF

12 OUNCES FRESH ASPARAGUS, TRIMMED AND CUT INTO 1-INCH PIECES (ABOUT 1½ CUPS; SEE NOTE; OPTIONAL)

4 TABLESPOONS BUTTER

2½ CUPS SLICED FRESH MUSHROOMS

1½ CUPS 1-INCH PIECES RED BELL PEPPER

⅓ CUP ALL-PURPOSE FLOUR

2½ CUPS LOW-SODIUM OR REGULAR CHICKEN BROTH

1½ CUPS HALF-AND-HALF OR CREAM

½ CUP DRY SHERRY (OR ADDITIONAL CHICKEN BROTH)

1½ TEASPOONS LEMON ZEST

4 CUPS CHOPPED OR SHREDDED COOKED CHICKEN OR TURKEY

1½ CUPS SHREDDED OR GRATED PARMESAN CHEESE

2 TABLESPOONS CHOPPED FRESH OR 2 TEASPOONS DRIED PARSLEY

GROUND SEA OR KOSHER SALT

GROUND BLACK PEPPER

GARNISH: CHOPPED FRESH OR DRIED PARSLEY (OPTIONAL)

---

1 Preheat the oven to 375°F.

2 Cook the vermicelli in boiling water. Three minutes before its suggested cooking time, add the asparagus (if using) and let cook for 1 minute. At that point, check the pasta to see if it's al dente (see "Use Your Noodle", page 31). If so, drain it along with the asparagus (but don't rinse the pasta with water).

3 Add the pasta-asparagus mixture to a large bowl, reserving 6 to 8 asparagus tips in a small bowl for garnish.

4 In a large skillet over medium-low heat, melt 1½ tablespoons of the butter. Add the mushrooms and bell pepper, stirring frequently, until the vegetables are tender, 5 to 7 minutes. Drain the mixture and add it to the pasta-asparagus mixture, reserving 6 to 8 mushroom slices for garnish.

5 Using the same large skillet, melt the remaining 2½ tablespoons butter. Stir in the flour until smooth, about 1 minute. Whisk in the broth, half-and-half, sherry, and lemon zest and bring to a light boil, stirring constantly. Lower the heat and add the chicken, ½ cup of the Parmesan, and the parsley. Stir to combine until thickened, bubbly, and smooth, 2 to 3 minutes. Season with salt and pepper. Pour the chicken mixture over the pasta mixture. Toss gently to coat.

6 Spoon the mixture into a greased 13-by-9-inch or 3-quart baking dish. Top the casserole with the reserved vegetable pieces and the remaining Parmesan.

7 Cover the casserole loosely with aluminum foil and bake for 25 to 30 minutes, or until it is heated through. If desired, to lightly brown the cheese in spots, place the casserole under the broiler for 1 or 2 minutes, watching it closely. Let it stand for 5 minutes and garnish with parsley, if desired, before serving.

NOTE: For the asparagus, I strongly advise you not to use canned (which are too mushy); use frozen only if they're not too thin and small, and they've been defrosted and drained well. Fresh asparagus will give this a much brighter look and taste.

Storage
This can be made up to 24 hours before cooking (just don't add the final layer of cheese until it's ready to go in the oven). Cooked and tightly covered, it will keep well in the refrigerator for several days and in the freezer for up to 3 months. See "Just Chill" (page 41) for more tips.

Supreme Chicken, Corn & Black Bean Enchiladas

SERVES 8-10

I call these supreme because they are supremely easy. And flavorful. And beautiful. That's why I make one batch to eat immediately and one batch to freeze (hence the doubled ingredients here, but you can halve this for a smaller serving). Serve the enchiladas on a bed of yellow Spanish rice and garnish 'til your heart's content.

2 TABLESPOONS VEGETABLE OIL OR OLIVE OIL

1 CUP DICED RED ONION

2 GARLIC CLOVES, MINCED OR PRESSED

2 CUPS SHREDDED COOKED CHICKEN

1 TO 2 TABLESPOONS FRESH LIME JUICE

2 TEASPOONS GARLIC POWDER

2 TEASPOONS SOUTHWESTERN SPICE BLEND (SEE NOTES)

TWO 14.5-OUNCE CANS FIRE-ROASTED DICED TOMATOES WITH GREEN CHILES (SEE NOTES)

ONE 15.5-OUNCE CAN BLACK BEANS, RINSED AND DRAINED

1 CUP FRESH OR FROZEN CORN, THAWED

1 TABLESPOON ALL-PURPOSE FLOUR

3 CUPS SHREDDED CHEDDAR-JACK CHEESE BLEND

½ TO 1 TEASPOON GROUND SEA OR KOSHER SALT

¼ TEASPOON GROUND BLACK PEPPER

TWENTY 6-INCH CORN TORTILLAS (SEE NOTES)

TWO 19-OUNCE CANS RED ENCHILADA SAUCE

GARNISH: CHOPPED FRESH CILANTRO, SOUR CREAM, DICED TOMATOES, AND/OR SLICED GREEN ONIONS

1 Preheat the oven to 350°F.

2 In a large skillet over medium heat, add the vegetable oil and sauté the onion and garlic until tender, about 5 minutes. Lower the heat and add the chicken. Sprinkle on the lime juice, garlic powder, and spice blend and cook, stirring occasionally, for 1 to 2 minutes to coat the chicken evenly. Add the tomatoes, beans, and corn. Stir gently to combine (so not to mash beans).

3 Lightly sprinkle the flour atop the mixture and let it simmer for about 1 minute before stirring; let simmer 2 minutes more. Add 1 cup of the cheese and stir. Remove from the heat and set aside. Season with the salt and pepper.

[CONTINUED]

4 Place a stack of tortillas in between two wet paper towels on a microwave-safe plate. Microwave them on high for about 45 seconds. (This will help make them more pliable.)

5 Coat two 13-by-9-inch baking dishes with nonstick cooking spray. Evenly pour 1 cup of the enchilada sauce across the bottom of each dish (using 2 cups total).

6 In a large shallow bowl, use tongs to dip each tortilla in the remaining enchilada sauce to lightly coat. Place the tortilla on a plate and spoon about ¼ cup of the chicken mixture at the edge. Gently roll it over the filling and place the enchilada seam-side down in the pan. Repeat with the remaining mixture and tortillas. Top each dish with equal amounts of the remaining enchilada sauce and cheese. (Note: If you wind up with some leftover chicken mixture, refrigerate it or freeze it to make quesadillas another night.)

7 Cover loosely in a slightly tented fashion with aluminum foil and bake for 25 minutes, or until the cheese melts and the sauce is bubbly. Uncover and bake 5 minutes more, lightly broiling the top of the casserole if you'd like the cheese and tortilla edges more golden. Serve with the garnishes, as desired.

NOTES: I like Emeril's Essence (see Sources, page 167). If you can't find what you need, use a mix of cumin, chili powder, and dried oregano.

If you can't find fire-roasted tomatoes with chiles, add fire-roasted tomatoes plus two 4-ounce cans fire-roasted diced green chiles.

Corn tortillas will stay moist while they bake if first dredged in enchilada sauce or chicken broth. Also, to keep enchiladas snuggled together (and not unrolling), station a small coffee cup in front of the rolled ones, moving it farther out each time you add another enchilada. And to help keep the tortilla edges from getting too dry and crisp, coat their ends with cooking spray just before you pop them into the oven.

Storage

These should be made just before baking to ensure the tortillas don't get soggy. Once cooked and tightly wrapped, they will keep in the refrigerator for several days. To freeze, don't cook them. Cover them with enchilada sauce, omit the final layer of cheese, and keep in an airtight container for up to 1 month. Defrost overnight and add the cheese just before baking. They'll be a bit more tamale-like in texture but still delicious. See "Just Chill" (page 41) for more tips.

Easy-Bake Chicken 'n' Herbed Dumplings

SERVES 6

You can fortify and fancify this by adding vegetables like green peas and carrots and whatnot, but to my way of thinking, that takes you more into pot-pie territory. This dish should just basically be creamy-rich chicken and flavorful dumplings. For whatever reason, I never really cottoned to the dish until I met my husband-to-be (this book's photographer), who loves it. Each time we'd visit our relatives in Natchez, Mississippi, we'd be treated not only to his mother Edith's version of it, but his Aunt Colleen Groves' take on it, and his childhood home would be chicken 'n' dumpling central. This is my quick-cooking tribute to those fun days.

3 TABLESPOONS BUTTER

½ CUP FINELY CHOPPED ONION

½ CUP FINELY CHOPPED CELERY

1 GARLIC CLOVE, MINCED

½ CUP ALL-PURPOSE FLOUR

1½ TEASPOONS DRIED FINES HERBES (SEE NOTES)

ONE 16-OUNCE CARTON CHICKEN BROTH (SEE NOTES)

TWO 10.75-OUNCE CANS CREAM OF CHICKEN SOUP (SEE NOTES)

4 CUPS SHREDDED OR CHOPPED COOKED CHICKEN

¼ TO ½ TEASPOON GROUND SEA OR KOSHER SALT (SEE NOTES)

¼ TEASPOON GROUND BLACK PEPPER

HERBED DUMPLINGS

2 CUPS SELF-RISING FLOUR OR BISCUIT/BAKING MIX

2 TEASPOONS DRIED FINES HERBES OR DRIED TARRAGON AND/OR ROSEMARY

1¼ CUPS BUTTERMILK, WHOLE MILK, HALF-AND-HALF, OR CREAM

2 TABLESPOONS BUTTER, MELTED

GARNISH: DRIED FINES HERBES, TARRAGON, ROSEMARY, OR PARSLEY

1 Preheat the oven to 350°F.

2 In a large saucepan, melt the butter over medium heat and sauté the onion, celery, and garlic until tender, 5 to 7 minutes. Add the flour and fines herbes and stir until blended.

3 Slowly add the broth, soup, and then the chicken and bring the mixture to a boil, stirring until the sauce is thickened, 2 to 3 minutes. Taste the mixture and add the salt and pepper; adjust the seasoning as desired.

[CONTINUED]

4 Pour the chicken mixture into a greased 13-by-9-inch dish and set aside.

TO MAKE THE DUMPLINGS

5 In a medium bowl, combine the flour and fines herbes. Slowly add the buttermilk and stir with a fork until moistened, smooth, and just combined (don't over-work the dough or it can get tough). Use a small cookie scoop or tablespoon to drop 12 rounded batter portions over the chicken mixture in the casserole dish.

6 Bake, uncovered, for 25 minutes (the dumplings will have a light crust). Remove the casserole and brush the tops of the dumplings with the melted butter. Cover loosely and bake 7 to 10 minutes longer, or until a tooth-pick inserted into a dumpling comes out clean. Broil the dumpling tops to make them more golden, if desired. Garnish with fines herbes before serving.

NOTES: Instead of fines herbes, you can substitute a desired mix of dried rosemary, tarragon, and/or sage or use 1 teaspoon poultry seasoning.

Consider using reduced-sodium broth and/or cream of chicken soup, which lets you control the salt content to your liking (especially since prepared rotisserie chicken can be saltier than home-cooked chicken).

Salt should be added only after tasting the creamy chicken mixture.

Double the amount of dumplings if you know people will want extras. Just use another casserole dish with an extra can of cream of chicken soup poured in. Drop the second portion of dumplings there and cook using the same direc-tions outlined in step 6, but just check on your dumplings-only dish about 10 minutes sooner; they can cook faster.

Storage

This can be made up to 24 hours before cooking (just don't add the dumplings until it's ready to go in the oven). Cooked and tightly covered, the casserole will keep well in the refrig-erator for up to 3 days and in the freezer for up to 3 months (provided you freeze the dumplings separately). To reheat, cook the casserole filling in the oven and when it begins to bubble, add the frozen dumplings, cover with tented alu-minum foil, and allow them to thoroughly reheat. See "Just Chill" (page 41) for more tips.

King Ranch Chicken

SERVES 6–8

This dish could just as easily be in the "Company's Comin'" chapter because of how popular it is to cook for crowds. But it's such a down-home, easy-to-make recipe that I often make it on Sunday evenings just to have leftovers for dinner after a busy Monday. Some use flour tortillas in this, but I don't think they lend as much flavor (unless they're whole wheat or red chile–infused or the like); they also get mushy. Some add tortilla or corn chips on the bottom layer for added support, something I might try sometime. But this is the recipe for which I regularly get requests.

TWELVE 6-INCH CORN TORTILLAS

2 TABLESPOONS VEGETABLE OIL

1 CUP CHOPPED ONION

1 CUP CHOPPED GREEN BELL PEPPER

1 GARLIC CLOVE, MINCED

1 JALAPEÑO, SEEDED AND MINCED (OPTIONAL)

2 CUPS SHREDDED COOKED CHICKEN

ONE 10.75-OUNCE CAN CREAM OF CHICKEN OR MUSHROOM SOUP

ONE 10-OUNCE CAN DICED TOMATOES WITH GREEN CHILES (SUCH AS RO*TEL)

1 CUP SOUR CREAM

¼ CUP CHOPPED FRESH CILANTRO

1 TABLESPOON FRESH LIME JUICE

1½ TEASPOONS CHILI POWDER

¼ TEASPOON GROUND SEA OR KOSHER SALT

¼ TEASPOON GROUND BLACK PEPPER

2 CUPS SHREDDED CHEDDAR-JACK CHEESE BLEND

GARNISH: CHOPPED CILANTRO, TOMATOES, AND/OR GREEN ONION SLICES

1 Preheat the oven to 350°F.

2 Tear the tortillas into 1-inch pieces and set aside.

3 In a large skillet over medium-high heat, add the vegetable oil and sauté the onion, bell pepper, garlic, and jalapeño (if using) for about 5 minutes, or until tender.

4 Stir in the chicken, soup, tomatoes, sour cream, cilantro, lime juice, chili powder, salt, and pepper. Simmer, stirring occasionally, for about 3 minutes. Remove from the heat.

5 Layer one third of the tortilla pieces in the bottom of a greased 13-by-9-inch or 3-quart baking dish. Top with one-third of the chicken mixture and ⅔ cup of the cheese. Repeat the layers twice, making sure to cover the tortilla pieces well.

6 Bake covered for 30 minutes; uncover and cook for 5 minutes more, until the mixture is set and the cheese is completely melted. Serve with the garnishes.

NOTE: Use reduced-sodium soup, broth, low-fat cheese, and sour cream to make this dish and others more healthful for you. For similar tips, see "Do the Lighten Up," page 39.

Storage

Make this casserole the night before cooking it for the best flavor (don't add the final layer of cheese until just before baking). Cooked and tightly covered, it will keep well in the refrigerator for several days and in the freezer for up to 1 month. Let it thaw in the refrigerator before reheating. See "Just Chill" (page 41) for more tips.

LIL' DISH

KING RANCH . . . CHICKEN?

South Texas' famous King Ranch, which has claimed ginormous acreage between Corpus Christi and Brownsville since before the Civil War, is a cattle- and horse-breeding operation with farming ventures that does not, in fact, include chickens (though a few may be seen here or there). So how did the iconic Tex-Southern casserole take on the King Ranch name? It most likely happened in the 1950s, when canned soup came into prominence and this recipe began appearing. Some marketing person probably tacked the exotic-sounding ranch name onto a Western-style chicken dish and off it galloped into culinary history.

Hurry, Hooray Chicken Pot Pie

SERVES 6

Making good ol' chicken pot pie doesn't get any easier than this. This speedy recipe is an exceptional use for leftover rotisserie chicken. Now, for the slower-food version of this Southern classic, see page 109.

TWO 9-INCH FROZEN DEEP-DISH PIE CRUST SHELLS, THAWED (SEE NOTES)

3 CUPS FROZEN MIXED VEGETABLES OR TWO 15-OUNCE CANS MIXED VEGETABLES, WELL DRAINED

2½ CUPS DICED COOKED CHICKEN

ONE 10.75-OUNCE CAN CREAM OF CHICKEN SOUP (SEE NOTES)

ONE 10.75-OUNCE CAN CREAM OF CELERY SOUP (SEE NOTES)

1 TEASPOON ITALIAN HERB SEASONING

1 Preheat the oven to the recommended baking temperature for the pie crust. Prebake one of the crusts for the bottom of the pot pie until very lightly browned, 7 to 12 minutes (for more tips, see page 36); place the crust on a wire rack to cool.

2 Set the oven temperature to 350°F.

3 If using frozen vegetables, cook them for half the suggested cooking time; drain and set aside. In a medium bowl, gently combine the chicken with the vegetables, both soups, and Italian herb seasoning.

4 Pour the filling into the prebaked shell. Place the other pie crust atop the filling and seal the edges decoratively by pinching them closed or crimping. Cut slits in a desired pattern or, if you want to get fancier, before topping, remove sections with a large or small cookie cutter (like a leaf, star, chicken, or heart) to allow steam to release. (If desired, use an egg wash [see page 36] to give the crust sheen.)

5 Bake for 30 minutes, or until the filling is bubbly and the crust is golden. During the last 15 to 30 minutes of baking, cover the crust's edge with strips of aluminum foil to prevent excess browning. Let stand 10 minutes before serving.

NOTES: Instead of pie crust, consider using a 9-inch deep-dish pie plate and one of the suggested toppings on pages 35 to 36.

Using at least one low-sodium version of the soups, if not both, lets you better adjust the salt level of this dish, which can spike if your chicken is already well seasoned.

Storage

This should be assembled just before cooking or the pie crust will get soggy. Cooked and tightly covered, it will keep well in the refrigerator for up to 3 days and in the freezer for up to 2 months (that's if you don't use potatoes in your filling, which will turn into slush when frozen). See "Just Chill" (page 41) for more tips.

Fab Frito Pie

I'm fond of making this with leftover red or green chili, but you also can use good-quality canned chili to hasten the cooking time. Frito Pie is a guaranteed hit at any football-watching party or tailgate gathering (maybe 'cause it goes so well with beer). For a nostalgic (and disposable) presentation, empty out small, individual-size bags of chips (cut lengthwise at the side instead of at the top) and set the bags, with a plastic spoon in each, in a cloth-lined basket for use as serving vessels. Have each person grab a bag, scoop some of the casserole into it, and let them garnish as desired. It'll be just like having the Frito pies of high-school football game concession stand yore—but much tastier.

4 CUPS COOKED CHILI OR TWO 15-OUNCE CANS CHILI WITH BEEF (WITH OR WITH-OUT BEANS)	ONE 14-OUNCE, SEVEN 2-OUNCE, OR FOURTEEN 1-OUNCE BAGS FRITOS CORN CHIPS, PLUS MORE IF DESIRED	½ CUP SOUR CREAM
¼ CUP CHOPPED GREEN ONIONS	3 CUPS SHREDDED SHARP CHEDDAR OR CHEDDAR-JACK CHEESE	GARNISH: GREEN ONION SLICES, DICED TOMATOES, SHREDDED LETTUCE, AND/ OR JALAPEÑO SLICES

1 Preheat the oven to 350°F.

2 In a medium saucepan over medium heat, warm the chili and green onions, stirring occasionally, until hot, 5 to 7 minutes.

3 In a 2½-quart baking dish, evenly spread 3½ to 4 cups of the corn chips, pressing down to flatten them slightly. Pour half of the chili-onion mixture evenly over the chips and add half of the cheese.

4 Add another even layer of 3½ to 4 cups corn chips, using a spatula to press them down into the first layer, breaking and flattening them slightly. Top with the remaining chili-onion mixture and cheese.

5 Cover loosely with aluminum foil and bake for 20 minutes. Uncover the casserole and bake 5 minutes more, or until the cheese is melted and bubbly. Garnish as desired and serve.

Storage

This should be assembled just before cooking. Cooked and tightly covered, this will keep well in the refrigerator for up to 3 days. Freezing it will make its texture gooey, so I advise that you freeze leftover chili instead (which will keep for up to 4 months) and after thawing and reheating it on the stovetop, make this Frito pie. See "Just Chill" (page 41) for more tips.

LIL' DISH

FRITO OLÉ

Back in 1932, C. E. Doolin was so impressed by the flavor of a bag of corn chips he'd purchased at a San Antonio café, that he later bought the recipe—and the business—and began selling Fritos Corn Chips from his Model T Ford. The same year, about 935 miles away in Nashville, a snack-foods delivery man named Herman W. Lay bought out the company he was working for, forming the H. W. Lay & Company, which soon became one of the largest snack food companies in the Southeast. By 1961, Doolin and Lay had joined forces to form Frito-Lay, Inc. The company, now based in Dallas, has more than 45,000 employees and thirty-two different brands (including Cheetos, Doritos, Sun Chips, and Cracker Jack).

Lil' Tamale Pies

SERVES 4

This Tex-Mex quick pick-me-up is perfect for nights when you're hungry for flavor—
and fast. Plus, it'll make your kitchen smell like you've been cooking for ages.

1 POUND GROUND BULK PORK SAUSAGE (SEE NOTE)

ONE 10-OUNCE CAN DICED MEXICAN-STYLE OR REGULAR TOMATOES, WITH THEIR JUICES

½ CUP PITTED, SLICED GREEN OR BLACK OLIVES

ONE 1.25-OUNCE PACKET REDUCED-SODIUM TACO SEASONING

ONE 8.5-OUNCE PACKAGE CORN MUFFIN MIX

½ CUP SHREDDED CHEDDAR-JACK CHEESE BLEND, OR MORE AS DESIRED

GARNISH: SLICED OLIVES, SLICED CHERRY TOMATOES, SOUR CREAM, AND/OR CILANTRO (OPTIONAL)

1 Preheat the oven to 425°F.

2 In a large skillet, brown the sausage; remove it to a colander to drain while reserving 2 tablespoons drippings. Add the tomatoes with their juices, olives, and taco seasoning to the skillet. Cook, stirring occasionally, until heated through, about 5 minutes. Return the cooked, drained pork to the skillet and stir to combine. Adjust the seasoning as desired.

3 Prepare the corn muffin mix according to the package directions.

4 Divide the spiced pork mixture between four 12- to 16-ounce or 1½- to 2-cup casserole dishes. Top each with equal amounts of muffin mix; sprinkle with equal amounts of the cheese.

5 Bake the casseroles on a rimmed baking sheet for 15 minutes, or until the topping is light golden and cooked through. Garnish, if desired, before serving.

NOTE: Substitute 1 pound of ground beef for a milder or leaner filling. For a vegetarian option, use vegetable-blend crumbles or a mix of seasoned beans.

[CONTINUED]

Storage

The seasoned pork and cornbread batter can be prepared in advance; add the batter to each dish just before popping in the oven (noting it may take a little longer to cook if the ingredients are cold). Speaking of cold, make sure your individual casserole dishes are ovenproof or they'll crack if they go from cold to hot so quickly. Cooked and tightly wrapped, these will keep well in the refrigerator for up to 3 days or frozen for up to 3 months (just don't add the cheese until baking). See "Just Chill" (page 41) for more tips.

LIL' DISH

GRAND OLE MARTHA WHITE

There's White Lily (see page 38) and then there's another mill by the name of White, as in Martha. In 1899, Tennessean Richard Lindsey named his company's finest flour for his three-year-old daughter. Since then, Martha White has been making quality flour, cornmeal, grits, and baking mixes. Lindsey's Royal Flour Mill continued providing flour and cornmeal to the Nashville area before another Tennessee family sold their farm to go into the business. Being in "Music City," the company folks knew their customers liked country music nearly as much as they liked biscuits and cornbread, so Martha White's first advertising aired in the 1940s with their sponsorship of a 5:45 a.m. radio show, the "Martha White Biscuit and Cornbread Time." In 1948, they began sponsoring the Grand Ole Opry, and even today, Martha White remains the show's longest continuing sponsor.

GOT YOU COVERED

The kitchen is where all of us head for immediate comfort—not just for ourselves, but also for others. We cook there in times of joy and also in times of sorrow. It's the heart and hearth of Southern graciousness—which, at its best, is shared with others.

POT LUCKY

Potlucks, covered-dish dinners, church suppers, office parties—we're all asked to take something to one every now and then. Other than the person who brings a bucket of chicken (hey, it's all good . . . well, sometimes), or a package of already-opened, stale cookies (OK, that's not so good), the rest of us are in one-upmanship mode, quietly watching to see whose dish gets devoured first (though we'd never, ever admit that, of course).

To know which dishes *do* get devoured most often, here are the top ten winningest ones based on a highly unscientific but well-intentioned Facebook poll of Southern foodies, friends, and family:

1 Chicken casseroles or pot pies

2 Lasagna

3 Whole or half honey-glazed ham

4 Deviled eggs

5 Macaroni 'n' cheese

6 Fried chicken

7 Meat loaf

8 Bread pudding

9 Scones, muffins, or cinnamon rolls

10 A layer or sheet cake (chocolate or red velvet elicit the most joy)

Baked Spaghetti

SERVES 6-8

Others may think of this dish as a slap-together concoction of leftovers, but down South, it's taken quite seriously. It's a mainstay at fundraisers, potlucks, and church suppers. This is a layered version, which is more attractive, but you can easily just do it up mix-and-melt style. If you plan to use commercially made sauce, just make sure it's good quality, since it'll have a big effect on this dish's flavor.

12 OUNCES DRIED SPAGHETTI (SEE NOTES)

1 POUND GROUND BULK ITALIAN SAUSAGE (SEE NOTES)

1 CUP FINELY CHOPPED ONION

6 CUPS GO-TO MARINARA SAUCE (PAGE 27) OR TWO 24-OUNCE JARS MARINARA SAUCE (SEE NOTES)

½ TEASPOON ITALIAN HERB SEASONING

⅓ CUP SHREDDED PARMESAN CHEESE

2 EGGS

3 TABLESPOONS BUTTER, MELTED

2 CUPS RICOTTA CHEESE (SEE NOTES)

3 TO 4 CUPS SHREDDED ITALIAN BLEND CHEESE

GARNISH: DRIED RED PEPPER FLAKES, FRESH PARSLEY LEAVES (OPTIONAL)

1 Preheat the oven to 350°F.

2 Break the spaghetti into smaller pieces (perhaps three 4-inch sections) and cook it in boiling water. Two minutes before its suggested cooking time, check to see if it's al dente (see "Use Your Noodle," page 31). If so, drain the pasta (but don't rinse it with water) and set it aside.

3 Meanwhile, in a large skillet, cook the sausage and onion over medium heat until the meat is no longer pink; drain and return it to the skillet. Stir in the marinara sauce and Italian herb seasoning; set aside.

4 In a large bowl, whisk together the Parmesan, eggs, and butter. Add the spaghetti and toss to coat.

5 Spread half of the coated spaghetti mixture into a lightly greased 13-by-9-inch baking dish. Top with half of the ricotta, sausage-marinara sauce, and Italian blend cheese. Repeat the layers once more.

6 Cover loosely and bake at 350°F for 40 minutes. Uncover and bake for 15 to 20 minutes longer, or until the cheese is melted and bubbly. Garnish with red pepper flakes and parsley leaves, if desired, before serving.

[CONTINUED]

Soul Food with a Cornbread Cap

SERVES 6-8

This has every soul-comforting ingredient you could possibly put in one dish, and it's made scrumptious with a cornbread topping. Serve this with your favorite bottle of pepper sauce. (Which just might be your own; see "Get Sauced: Pickled Peppers," page 88.)

3 TABLESPOONS VEGETABLE OIL

4 CUPS DICED COOKED HAM

¼ CUP ALL-PURPOSE FLOUR

1 QUART CHICKEN BROTH

2 CUPS FROZEN YOUNG LIMA BEANS, THAWED, OR ONE 15-OUNCE CAN YOUNG LIMA BEANS, RINSED AND WELL DRAINED

ONE 16-OUNCE PACKAGE FROZEN CHOPPED COLLARD GREENS

ONE 12-OUNCE PACKAGE FROZEN SEASONING BLEND (SEE NOTE)

ONE 15-OUNCE CAN BLACK-EYED PEAS, RINSED AND WELL DRAINED

1 TEASPOON CAJUN SEASONING

½ TEASPOON GARLIC POWDER

½ TEASPOON GROUND SEA OR KOSHER SALT

¼ TEASPOON CAYENNE PEPPER (OPTIONAL)

TWO 6.5-OUNCE PACKAGES YELLOW CORNBREAD MIX

HOT PEPPER VINEGAR OR OTHER HOT SAUCE (OPTIONAL)

1 Preheat the oven to 425°F.

2 In a Dutch oven, heat the vegetable oil over medium-high heat and add the ham; sauté until lightly browned, about 5 minutes. Add the flour, and stirring constantly to absorb the oil, cook it for about 30 seconds. Gradually add the broth and cook, stirring constantly, until it begins to thicken, about 4 minutes.

3 Bring the mixture to a boil and immediately add the frozen lima beans (if using), collard greens, and seasoning blend; return to a boil and cook, stirring often, for 15 minutes.

4 Carefully stir in the canned lima beans (if using instead of frozen), black-eyed peas, Cajun seasoning, garlic powder, salt, and cayenne pepper (if using); spoon the hot mixture into a lightly greased 2½- to 3-quart baking dish.

5 Prepare the cornbread according to the package directions and pour the batter evenly over the ham-vegetable mixture.

6 Bake for about 25 minutes, or until the cornbread is golden brown and set. Remove from the oven and let cool for 8 to 10 minutes before serving with hot pepper vinegar, if desired.

[CONTINUED]

NOTE: Frozen seasoning blend is a mix of diced onion, celery, and bell pepper. It's as common in Southern freezers as ice.

Storage

This can be made up to 1 day before cooking (just don't add the cornbread topping until just before baking). Cooked and tightly covered, it will keep well in the refrigerator for several days and frozen for up to 3 months. See "Just Chill" (page 41) for more tips.

LIL' DISH

GET SAUCED: PICKLED PEPPERS

For a sidekick, I pickle my own peppers and keep them in old liquor bottles fitted with a lidded pouring spout (like the kind they use in bars). First, make sure your bottle is very clean. Wear gloves to handle a good handful (3 to 4 ounces) of thin serrano, jalapeño, Fresno, cayenne, Holland, and/or Thai chile peppers (ones that'll easily slip though the bottle opening, yet won't be too hot). Slice them vertically with a paring knife, carefully scraping out the seeds if desired, trying to keep the shapes intact. In a microwave-safe container (such as a large Pyrex measuring cup), cook 3 to 4 cups of distilled or white wine vinegar on high until it comes to a boil, about 6 minutes. Remove it from the microwave and carefully add the chiles, along with a few garlic cloves and, if desired, some peppercorns. Use a thick wad of heavy-duty aluminum foil to help press the chiles down into the vinegar (they'll want to float) and get them fully saturated. (You may have to place a small heavy object like a mallet on top of the foil to further weigh it down.) Cover the mixture as well as possible and let it cool to room temperature (several

hours). Wear gloves again and use a funnel to pour the pepper-infused vinegar into the liquor bottle. Insert the peppers and garlic cloves into the bottle. Add the lidded pour spout and keep the pepper sauce refrigerated. It will keep well for up to 4 months.

When Southerners know you are hurting, either from illness or the loss of a loved one, they'll start showing up to your house with care packages almost as soon as they hear the news. Everything's appreciated, but everyone should consider these tips:

+ Besides taking a comforting dish, ask if there's anything else the person really needs (soft drinks, paper plates, plastic cups and utensils, garbage bags, etc.) so you might bring a little something extra (or only those things).

+ Consider making, buying, or having catered a complete dinner, from the main dish to dessert. Our family often chips in for barbecue chicken, brisket, pulled pork, and/or sausage, with a few side dishes, a loaf of bread, and maybe some hand pies. It's nice when a friend or two can also pitch in on the expense to make it a shared gift that will last for a while.

+ If you're not close friends with a person who is ill, but still want to do something nice for him or her, ask a mutual friend what food allergies or other food issues you should know about; perhaps the person is diabetic or on a special health-related diet.

+ If you know the food will be eaten right away, take something precooked and ready to be reheated. Have it in a container that will allow for easy reheating (and disposal, if possible).

+ If the family will be in and out of their home for various reasons, take them something frozen that can be defrosted and enjoyed at their convenience.

SELF-PRESERVATION

I'm sure *anything* would be appreciated, but please don't follow in the footsteps of one of my grandmother's friends, who'd bring us one of her "famous" fruitcakes, which tasted as if it had been frozen for a century. I picture all of them now in a landfill near Natchez, Mississippi, sadly looking exactly as they did forty years ago.

CHAPTER 03

Company's Comin'

If we couldn't share our mutual love of food, storytelling, togetherness, and tabletop finery, then what on Earth would we ever do with ourselves? Entertaining is essential to happiness. So are these luxe main-dish casseroles that leave a lasting impression, with truly very little effort. These are the recipes that bring out the very best of Southern ingredients—and the very best in us.

For Starters . . . Classic Southern Spreads

When it comes to party appetizers served casserole style, here are four Southern favorites I adore. (The Artichoke & Parmesan Dip is pictured at right.) Serve them with unseasoned crackers, toasted French baguette slices, tortilla chips, toasted pita wedges or chips, and/or sliced vegetables. Many of these dishes can be made a day ahead and slowly reheated before your gathering. Just avoid freezing them; mayo and cream cheese don't fare well at arctic temps.

Crème de la Crab

SERVES 4–6

8 ounces cream cheese

1 cup sour cream

½ cup shredded sharp Cheddar cheese

¼ cup mayonnaise

3 tablespoons whole milk, or more for desired consistency

2 tablespoons cream sherry

1 tablespoon Worcestershire sauce

1 teaspoon dry mustard

½ teaspoon fresh lemon juice

¼ teaspoon garlic salt

1 pound fresh lump crabmeat, well picked

Garnish: Lemon zest

Add the cream cheese and sour cream to a medium, microwave-safe bowl and heat on defrost power for 4½ minutes. Use a whisk to combine well. Add the Cheddar, mayonnaise, milk, sherry, Worcestershire, mustard, lemon juice, and garlic salt. Gently fold in the crabmeat. Heat the mixture in the top of a double boiler until hot and serve in a chafing dish to keep warm. Garnish with the lemon zest before serving.

Artichoke & Parmesan Dip

SERVES 4–6

Two 14-ounce cans artichoke hearts, drained and chopped

¾ cup light mayonnaise

2 tablespoons fresh lemon juice

2 garlic cloves, minced

1¼ cups grated Parmesan cheese

Garnish: Lemon zest

Preheat the oven to 350°F. Combine the artichoke hearts, mayonnaise, lemon juice, garlic, and 1 cup of the Parmesan and spoon them into a lightly greased 1-quart baking dish. Sprinkle with the remaining Parmesan. Bake uncovered for 30 minutes, or until bubbly and lightly browned. Garnish with the lemon zest before serving.

Black-Eyed Pea Hummus

SERVES 4–6

1 tablespoon butter

1 medium sweet onion, thinly sliced

½ teaspoon sugar

One 15-ounce can black-eyed peas, rinsed and drained (a few reserved for garnish)

1 tablespoon olive oil

1 tablespoon sesame oil

1 garlic clove

½ teaspoon minced fresh rosemary

½ teaspoon ground sea or kosher salt

¼ teaspoon ground black pepper

6 tablespoons shredded Asiago cheese

Garnish: Reserved black-eyed peas, fresh rosemary sprig(s)

Preheat the oven to 400°F. In a large skillet, melt the butter over medium heat. Add the onion and sugar and reduce the heat to medium-low. Cook, stirring often, until the onion is very soft and caramelized, 22 to 25 minutes. Coarsely chop and set aside.

In the bowl of a food processor, combine the black-eyed peas, olive oil, sesame oil, garlic, rosemary, salt, and pepper. Add 2 tablespoons water and process until smooth. Stir in 2 tablespoons of the Asiago.

Spoon the mixture into a 12- to 16-ounce casserole dish. Top with the caramelized onion and remaining 4 tablespoons Asiago. Bake for 15 to 20 minutes, or until the cheese is golden and the hummus is heated through. Garnish with a few black-eyed peas placed at the base of one or two rosemary sprigs before serving.

Walnut Stilton Torta

SERVES 10

This woo-worthy recipe from Susan Smith Ellard is adapted from *Tables of Content: Service, Settings and Supper* by the Junior League of Birmingham (see page 107).

2½ tablespoons butter, plus ½ cup, softened

½ cup chopped walnuts

¼ cup packed light brown sugar

⅛ teaspoon ground sea or kosher salt

Two 8-ounce packages cream cheese, softened

¼ cup port or other sweet red wine (see Notes)

1½ cups crumbled Clemson or Stilton blue cheese (see Notes)

1 cup seedless raspberry jam, at room temperature

Garnish: 1 bunch red grapes, thinly sliced green onions

French bread slices, toasted

In a small skillet, melt the 2½ tablespoons butter over medium heat. Add the walnuts, brown sugar, and salt and cook, stirring frequently, until the brown sugar dissolves and the mixture is bubbly (about 5 minutes). Evenly spread the candied walnut mixture on parchment paper and let it cool (about 10 minutes) before breaking it into pieces.

In a medium mixing bowl, use an electric mixer set on medium speed to combine the cream cheese and ½ cup softened butter. Add the wine and whip until smooth.

Use plastic wrap to line a small ring mold or round bowl that can hold at least 3½ cups.

Spread 1 cup of the cream cheese–wine mixture into the prepared mold and sprinkle with ¾ cup of the blue cheese. Spread with ½ cup of the jam and sprinkle with one-third of the candied walnuts.

Layer with 1 cup of the remaining cream cheese–wine mixture, the remaining blue cheese and jam, and half of the remaining candied walnuts. Top with the last of the cream cheese mixture.

Chill, tightly covered with plastic wrap, for 8 hours or until set. Invert the torta onto a serving platter and sprinkle with the last of the candied walnuts. Garnish with the grapes and green onions and serve with toasted French bread slices.

NOTES: Concord grape or cranberry juice may be substituted for the wine.

To order Clemson blue cheese, see page 167.

LIL' DISH

DUKE'S SUCCESS IS SPREADING

Mayonnaise is as Southern as egg salad on toast, baked artichoke dip (see page 92), and mayonnaise cake. And there's no mayo more Southern than Duke's, whose mayonnaise has long been a mainstay in the Carolinas, and which has an ever-growing cult following, even nationally. Some people could've seen that coming down Main Street.

Back in 1917, an enterprising Eugenia Duke of Greenville, South Carolina, began selling sandwiches at nearby Fort Sevier. Her homemade mayo really got to the fellas and their loved ones and the base workers and *their* loved ones, and pretty soon the locals were in a tizzy for it. She ultimately went from selling several dozen sandwiches daily to 11,000 in one day. Seeing a good thing when they tasted it, in 1929 the C. F. Sauer company purchased her business and she became its chief salesperson, handing off the business particulars to them while she could work as their chief promoter.

Eugenia would be pleased to know that at last check, *BusinessWeek* listed Duke's mayonnaise as one of the nation's top fifteen bestselling condiments. Check retailers or buy online at DukesMayo.com.

Oysters Rockefeller en Casserole

In honor of how oysters Rockefeller is most often seen—in oyster shells—I enlist small ramekins to host this anise-tinged New Orleans classic. Without creating attractive serving-vessel diversions, the gooey green-gray-beige concoction is simply more ooh-aah to eat than, well, look at. As a side dish, it's delightful alongside prime rib during the fall holiday season, when oysters are at their plumpest (as are many of us). As an appetizer casserole, this recipe is hugely popular in the Gulf states, where it's served in elegant chafing dishes (see page 126) and scooped onto toasted baguette slices.

24 FRESHLY SHUCKED OYSTERS

½ CUP BUTTER

½ CUP FINELY CHOPPED ONION

¼ CUP FINELY CHOPPED CELERY

2 TEASPOONS MINCED GARLIC

ONE 10-OUNCE PACKAGE FROZEN CHOPPED SPINACH, THAWED AND DRAINED

½ CUP CHOPPED FRESH PARSLEY

1 TABLESPOON PERNOD LIQUEUR OR ¼ TEASPOON ANISEEDS

1½ TEASPOONS MINCED FRESH OR ½ TEASPOON DRIED THYME

½ TEASPOON WORCESTERSHIRE SAUCE

⅛ TEASPOON CAYENNE PEPPER

GROUND BLACK PEPPER

GROUND SEA OR KOSHER SALT

1 CUP FRESHLY GRATED PARMESAN CHEESE

½ CUP PLAIN PANKO OR SOFT FRESH BREAD CRUMBS

GARNISH: FRESH THYME SPRIGS

1 Preheat the oven to 350°F.

2 Rinse and drain the oysters and keep them refrigerated until ready for use.

3 In a large skillet, melt the butter and sauté the onion, celery, and garlic. Cook until soft, 5 to 7 minutes. Stir in the spinach, parsley, Pernod, thyme, Worcestershire, and cayenne and season with black pepper and salt.

4 Grease eight 6-ounce ramekins.

5 Place 3 oysters at the base of each ramekin and top evenly with the spinach mixture.

6 Place the filled ramekins on a rimmed baking sheet and bake for 30 minutes.

7 Remove the ramekins and evenly top them with Parmesan and panko.

8 Return the ramekins to the oven and bake for 10 to 12 minutes more, until the cheese is melted and the bread crumbs are golden. Garnish with the thyme sprigs before serving.

Storage

The oysters can be topped with the spinach mixture and kept tightly covered in the refrigerator for up to 8 hours before baking as directed. Once baked, they will keep refrigerated for about 1 day. This would not freeze well.

THE LEGACY OF ANTOINE'S

ANTOINE'S RESTAURANT, 713 St. Louis St., NEW ORLEANS

As the nation's oldest family-run restaurant—in business since 1840—Antoine's is the namesake of Marseilles-born Antoine Alciatore. The French chef-restaurateur tried unsuccessfully to establish a restaurant in New York City before setting his sights on New Orleans' French Quarter. It was there that his French cooking artfully merged with his environs and what would become Creole cuisine was born. Oysters Rockefeller was created in 1899 by Antoine's son, Jules, who named his rich spinach-oyster recipe after America's richest man, John D. Rockefeller. (And had there not been a snail shortage at the time, it would have been Snails Rockefeller.) To enjoy the iconic dish in its elegant birthplace is a true thrill. (For more, visit Antoines.com.)

Seafood Supreme Pot Pies

There's pot pie . . . and then there's *this*. Chock-full of seafood, this is an edible version of John Coltrane's "A Love Supreme." Delicate wisps of buttery phyllo pastry piled atop each individual casserole makes breaking into these one of life's special pleasures—especially with a cool glass of Viognier white wine within reach.

2 TABLESPOONS UNSALTED BUTTER, PLUS ½ CUP	2 TO 3 TABLESPOONS DRY SHERRY OR WHITE WINE (OPTIONAL BUT NICE)	1 POUND LUMP CRABMEAT, DRAINED, SHELL PIECES REMOVED
2 CUPS CHOPPED LEEKS (WHITE AND PALE GREEN PARTS ONLY; SEE NOTES)	1 TABLESPOON LEMON ZEST	8 OUNCES MEDIUM (41/50 COUNT) SHRIMP, PEELED AND DEVEINED
1 CUP DICED CELERY	2 TEASPOONS OLD BAY OR OTHER MILD SEAFOOD SEASONING	1 CUP FROZEN ENGLISH PEAS
1 CUP DICED CARROTS	1½ TEASPOONS FRESH MINCED OR ½ TEASPOON DRIED THYME	TEN 14-BY-9-INCH SHEETS FROZEN PHYLLO DOUGH, THAWED (SEE PAGE 35)
¼ CUP ALL-PURPOSE FLOUR	½ TEASPOON GROUND SEA OR KOSHER SALT	BUTTER-FLAVORED COOKING SPRAY (SEE NOTES)
2 CUPS PEELED, DICED RUSSET POTATOES	⅛ TEASPOON CAYENNE PEPPER	GARNISH: FRESH THYME SPRIGS
TWO 8-OUNCE BOTTLES CLAM JUICE		

1 Preheat the oven to 375°F.

2 In a large Dutch oven, melt the 2 tablespoons butter over medium heat. Add the leeks, celery, and carrots and cook until tender, 5 to 7 minutes. Add the flour and stir to combine. Add the potatoes, clam juice, sherry (if using), lemon zest, Old Bay, thyme, salt, and cayenne; bring the mixture to a boil. Cover, reduce the heat to low, and simmer 15 minutes, or until the potatoes are tender. Adjust the seasonings as desired and remove the pot from the heat.

3 In a small skillet, melt the remaining ½ cup butter over medium-low heat. Cook it for 3 to 4 minutes, stirring constantly, until the butter is golden brown and fragrant (but pay very close attention to it; don't allow it to burn). Stir the browned butter into the vegetable mixture and gently fold in the crabmeat, shrimp, and peas until just combined.

4 Evenly fill six 10-ounce casserole dishes with the seafood mixture and set aside.

5 Stack the phyllo sheets on a clean work space. Roll them up, starting at the longest side, and cut them into $\frac{1}{2}$-inch strips. Drop the strips into a large bowl and carefully fluff them to separate. Coat the strips with butter-flavored cooking spray and toss lightly. Carefully arrange the strips in nests atop the casseroles and lightly spray each topping.

6 Bake for 25 to 30 minutes, or until the mixture is hot and bubbly and the phyllo is golden brown. Garnish with thyme sprigs before serving.

NOTES: Leeks provide a sweeter, more complex flavor than onion; if you can't find them, substitute 1½ cups diced sweet onion and ½ cup minced shallots.

Butter-flavored spray helps keep the phyllo from crumbling (and saves calories), but melted butter may be carefully brushed on the sheets before slicing.

Storage

The seafood mixture can be made up to 8 hours in advance before adding it to the dishes and topping with the phyllo. Cooked and tightly covered, it will keep in the refrigerator for 1 day. The phyllo texture will soften but will crisp up once reheated in the oven. Because the seafood mixture has phyllo and potatoes, it will not freeze well.

Shrimp & Artichoke Casserole Bienvenu

SERVES 6

Personifying the French word *bienvenue*, meaning "welcome," is Marcelle Bienvenu, the celebrated "Queen of Cajun Cooking." Raised in St. Martinville, Louisiana, on the banks of the Bayou Teche, Marcelle has lived a deliciously full life, one documented in such books as *Who's Your Mama, Are You Catholic*, and *Can You Make a Roux?* Speaking of mamas, this casserole is akin to one of her mama's recipes that the family often served on Easter, Memorial Day, or the Fourth of July at their Vermillion Bay camp as a side to barbecued chicken, roasted lamb, or grilled anything. "I remember Mama also served it to the ladies when they played bridge or canasta," Marcelle recalls.

8 TABLESPOONS BUTTER

3 TABLESPOONS ALL-PURPOSE FLOUR

¾ CUP WHOLE MILK

¾ CUP CREAM OR HALF-AND-HALF

1 CUP FRESHLY GRATED PARMESAN CHEESE

¼ CUP CHOPPED FRESH PARSLEY

1 TEASPOON WORCESTERSHIRE SAUCE

½ TEASPOON HOT SAUCE (MARCELLE FAVORS TABASCO)

¼ TEASPOON GROUND SEA OR KOSHER SALT

¼ TEASPOON GROUND BLACK PEPPER

ONE 14-OUNCE CAN ARTICHOKE HEARTS, PACKED IN WATER, DRAINED AND CHOPPED

2 POUNDS MEDIUM-LARGE (36/40 COUNT) SHRIMP, COOKED, PEELED, AND DEVEINED

¾ CUP CHOPPED YELLOW ONION

½ CUP CHOPPED SWEET BELL PEPPER

½ CUP CHOPPED CELERY

8 OUNCES FRESH MUSHROOMS, SLICED

1 TEASPOON PAPRIKA

GARNISH: FRESHLY GRATED PARMESAN CHEESE, CHOPPED FRESH PARSLEY

1 Preheat the oven to 300°F.

2 In a large skillet, melt 3 tablespoons of the butter over medium heat. Stir in the flour. When blended, gradually add the milk and cream, stirring constantly until the mixture is thick and smooth. Add ½ cup of the cheese, the parsley, Worcestershire, hot sauce, salt, and pepper; stir to combine.

3 In a 2-quart baking dish, arrange the artichoke hearts as the bottom layer. Scatter the shrimp evenly over the artichokes.

4 In another large skillet, melt the remaining 5 tablespoons butter. Add the onion, bell pepper, and celery and sauté until soft, 5 to 7 minutes. Add the mushrooms and cook for 2 minutes. Spoon this vegetable mixture over the shrimp.

5 Pour the seasoned cream sauce atop the vegetable mixture and sprinkle with the paprika and remaining 1/2 cup cheese.

6 Bake uncovered for 30 minutes, or until hot and bubbly. Garnish with additional cheese and parsley before serving.

Storage

This can be made (without the final layer of cheese) and kept refrigerated and tightly covered up to 8 hours before cooking. Cooked, this will keep in an airtight container in the refrigerator for up to 2 days and frozen for up to 2 months. See "Just Chill" (page 41) for more tips.

See "Just Chill" (page 41) for more tips.

LIL' DISH

HOT FOR FLAVOR

Tabasco Pepper Sauce hails from south Louisiana's Avery Island (which technically is a salt dome and not an island, but that's another subject for another day). In the 1860s, it was created by food connoisseur and keen gardener Edmund McIlhenny after he'd successfully grown a batch of spicy peppers (*Capsicum frutescens*) with seeds he'd acquired from much farther south, most likely Mexico. His interest in the peppers' sprightly taste was more than just a dalliance: After the Civil War, accessibility to spices was limited—unless, of course, you made your own, which is exactly what he did to amp up the flavor of the mostly bland food that was then common.

After getting the recipe to his liking, he named it "Tabasco" after a Mexican Indian word meaning "place where the soil is humid" and/or "place of the oyster shell" (both of which are true of the area, just south of Lafayette). He then strained it into perfume-style bottles (to help it better sprinkle instead of pour), and sealed it with green wax. Within twenty years, he had a hit on his hands (demand for it came from as far as Europe). Some 150 years later, the business is still run by his descendants, and the sauce is labeled in twenty-two languages/dialects and sold in more than 160 countries and territories. The McIlhenny Company, which operates a nature preserve, is also a fun and beautiful place to visit. For more, visit Tabasco.com.

Chicken, Mushroom & Wild Rice Casserole

SERVES 6–8

This casserole's a given. Literally. It's one of those dishes you most expect to find on a buffet table or in the hands of someone with comfort food. Sometimes this is made with water chestnuts and/or pimientos. And sometimes it includes sharp Cheddar cheese. This simpler version is what makes me happiest. I think the mushrooms help bring out the earthy flavor of the wild rice, and the hint of sherry and curry give it Southern coastal flavor. Since all of us at one point or another have made this with canned soup and a quick-cooking rice blend, I thought I'd offer the option of making it fully from scratch—so it's even more special than it already is.

½ CUP SLICED OR SLIVERED ALMONDS

3 POUNDS BONELESS, SKINLESS CHICKEN BREASTS (ABOUT 3 WHOLE OR 6 HALVES)

1 CUP CHICKEN BROTH

1 CUP CHOPPED CELERY

1 CUP CHOPPED SWEET OR WHITE ONION

½ CUP DRY SHERRY

1 TEASPOON CURRY POWDER

½ TEASPOON GROUND SEA OR KOSHER SALT

1½ TABLESPOONS BUTTER

1 POUND FRESH SHIITAKE, BABY PORTO-BELLO, OR BUTTON MUSHROOMS, SLICED

1 RECIPE SEASONED LONG GRAIN & WILD RICE (RECIPE FOLLOWS) OR TWO 6-OUNCE PACKAGES LONG-GRAIN AND WILD RICE BLEND, COOKED

CREAM OF MUSHROOM SAUCE (PAGE 24) OR ONE 10.75-OUNCE CAN CREAM OF MUSHROOM SOUP

1 CUP SOUR CREAM

1½ CUPS SHREDDED ITALIAN BLEND CHEESE

GARNISH: CHOPPED FRESH ITALIAN PARSLEY

1   Preheat the oven to 350°F.

2   Bake the almonds in a single layer in a shallow pan for 4 to 6 minutes, or until toasted and fragrant, stirring half-way through. Remove them to a small bowl and set aside.

3   In a large skillet over medium heat, bring the chicken, broth, celery, onion, sherry, curry powder, and salt to a boil, 7 to 10 minutes. Flip the breasts, reduce the heat to low, cover, and simmer for 45 minutes more, until the chicken is cooked through and the flavors have thoroughly melded. Remove the pan from the heat. Strain (and reserve the broth for the rice).

4 Let the chicken cool for about 10 minutes before cutting it into bite-size pieces.

5 Using the same large saucepan, melt the butter and sauté the mushrooms until just tender; drain and set aside.

6 In a large bowl, stir to combine the chicken, mushrooms, rice, mushroom sauce, sour cream, and 1 cup of the cheese blend.

7 Lightly grease a 13-by-9-inch baking dish. Spoon the chicken and rice mixture into the dish and bake covered for 40 minutes.

8 Uncover the casserole. Top with the almonds and remaining ½ cup cheese blend and return to the oven for about 5 minutes more, until the cheese is bubbly. Garnish with parsley before serving.

Storage

Unbaked and tightly covered, this casserole will keep nicely—and even improve—in the refrigerator for up to 24 hours, and it will freeze well for about 1 month. (Either way, just don't add the final layer of cheese and almonds until the final 5 minutes of cooking.) Cooked, it will keep refrigerated in an airtight container for up to 3 days. See "Just Chill" (page 41) for more tips.

Seasoned Long Grain & Wild Rice

○—— **MAKES ABOUT 5 CUPS** ——○

2 cups chicken broth or reserved broth from cooking chicken

1 cup long-grain white or brown rice (see Note)

½ cup wild rice

1 tablespoon fines herbes or herbes de Provence

½ teaspoon ground sea or kosher salt

In a medium saucepan, bring the broth and 1½ cups water to a boil. Add the long-grain and wild rices, fines herbes, and salt; stir to combine. Cover, reduce the heat, and simmer for 35 to 40 minutes, until the liquid is absorbed and the rice mixture is tender.

Remove the rice from heat, and let it sit, covered, for 10 minutes, before fluffing with a fork. Adjust the seasoning as desired before using as directed or serving as a side.

NOTE: Long-grain brown rice will take about 10 minutes longer to cook.

Country Captain Chicken

SERVES 4

This uniquely Southern chicken dish reportedly sailed into our lives when a British spice trade captain found himself in Savannah, Georgia, in the early 1800s. The story goes that his love of Indian food, and great distance from it, made him pine for chicken curry. And some cook somewhere in that diversely populated port city re-created something akin to this. Whether this is true I don't know, but I'm happy to believe it. This *is* mysteriously exotic for Southern fare then and even now—with tender chicken swaddled in sweet tomatoes, paprika, curry, currants, and nuts—sometimes even shredded coconut and mango (fresh or chutney). It's one of the most fun dishes you can serve company, especially since everyone can personalize their dish. And perhaps, after a glass or two of wine, they can embellish that sea captain's tale even more.

½ CUP DRIED CURRANTS OR GOLDEN RAISINS

¼ CUP FRESH ORANGE JUICE

ONE 3- TO 4-POUND CHICKEN, CUT INTO 8 PIECES

1 TABLESPOON SWEET PAPRIKA

1½ TEASPOONS GROUND SEA OR KOSHER SALT

1 TEASPOON GROUND BLACK PEPPER

1 TABLESPOON MINCED FRESH OR 1 TEASPOON DRIED THYME

1 CUP ALL-PURPOSE FLOUR

¼ CUP PEANUT OIL

6 BACON SLICES

1 CUP CHOPPED CELERY

1 CUP CHOPPED GREEN BELL PEPPER

1 CUP CHOPPED SWEET OR YELLOW ONION

3 GARLIC CLOVES, MINCED

ONE 28-OUNCE CAN STEWED OR DICED TOMATOES, WITH THEIR JUICES

2 TO 3 TABLESPOONS CURRY POWDER

2 TABLESPOONS BUTTER

2 BAY LEAVES

6 CUPS COOKED BASMATI RICE

GARNISH: CURRANTS AND CRUMBLED BACON; TOASTED SLIVERED OR SLICED ALMONDS, OR HALVED CASHEWS OR PEANUTS; SHREDDED COCONUT; CHOPPED FRESH MANGO OR MANGO CHUTNEY

1 Preheat the oven to 325°F.

2 Place the currants in a medium bowl and cover with the orange juice and $\frac{1}{2}$ cup warm water. Set aside for at least 30 minutes or make ahead and refrigerate before use.

3 Rinse the chicken pieces and pat them dry. Season with the paprika, salt, pepper, and thyme. Lightly dredge the seasoned pieces in the flour, shaking off any excess.

4 In a 5-quart Dutch oven, heat the peanut oil over high heat. Add the chicken, skin-side down, and cook for 5 to 7 minutes per side, until both sides are golden brown. Use tongs to place the chicken on a platter; cover with aluminum foil and set aside.

5 Discard the chicken drippings and return the Dutch oven to medium heat. Add the bacon and cook, stirring occasionally, until crisp, 6 to 8 minutes. Use tongs to remove the bacon onto paper towels to drain; leave the drippings in the pot.

6 Add the celery, bell pepper, onion, and garlic to the bacon drippings and cook, stirring occasionally, until soft, 8 to 10 minutes. Add the tomatoes with their juices, using kitchen shears to cut up any large pieces of tomatoes if using a stewed variety.

7 Drain and discard the liquid from the plumped currants and add them to the tomato mixture. Reduce the heat to medium-low and stir in the curry powder, butter, and bay leaves. Stir often but carefully (so as not to break up the bay leaves), until the sauce begins to thicken, 9 to 11 minutes. Adjust the seasonings as desired.

8 Add the reserved chicken to the pot, cradling it within the sauce, which should cover it. Bake, covered, for 1 hour and 15 minutes, or until the chicken is very tender. Remove the bay leaves, spoon the sauce and chicken atop the rice, and garnish as desired before serving.

Storage

The sauce can be made up to 1 day before searing the chicken and adding it for baking. Cooked and tightly covered, the casserole will keep in the refrigerator for several days and frozen (ungarnished, without rice) for up to 3 months. See "Just Chill" (page 41) for more tips.

SPIRAL-BOUND ROYALTY (AND THEN SOME)

Each time I open *Charleston Receipts*, I think about Country Captain Chicken and the time I asked my grandmother to cook it with me one weekend night. As a fellow culinary adventurer, she accepted the challenge, but I'll never forget the look on our A&P store manager's face when we inquired about mango chutney. (Insert confusion here.) Not to worry, Nannie said, we'll use some of her homemade Jezebel sauce instead. It was a good call. After cooking the dish, the house was never so fragrant, and we both felt quite sophisticated, if slightly unsure of what we were about to eat. Until we ate it. And felt transported to the Far East—which, at least as far as the South is concerned, is the coastal Lowcountry.

As the oldest Junior League cookbook in existence, *Charleston Receipts* was first published in 1950. It's the "bible" of such books, with some 800,000 copies in print. It's a true slice of yesteryear Americana, since many of its recipes were influenced by Lowcountry cooks who spoke the centuries-old coastal Gullah (Creole-style) language, which, through words and illustrations, is sprinkled throughout the 376 illustrated pages (with an unheard-of 750 recipes). Junior League cookbooks and other self-published cookbooks used to be homespun and spiral-bound until they became sleek and savvy.

Receipt vs. *recipe*—both words, deriving from the Latin *recipere*, or "to receive," share an interesting story: A "receipt," a British phrase traceable to the Middle Ages, originally referred to a doctor's prescription (which ultimately morphed into short form as an uppercase "R" with a slash through its descending right leg). Thus, any formula or set of directions that was good for you was known as a "receipt," but began being used interchangeably with its

French counterpart, "récipe," in the eighteenth century. In this country, people of English heritage, especially along the Atlantic coast, actually favored "receipt" until the 1970s. And many in Britain and Australia still use "receipt" out of respect for tradition.

Charleston Receipts is a treasure to me. Other books equally cherished for Southern storytelling and foodways include, in the order of their publication:

RIVER ROAD RECIPES: THE TEXTBOOK OF LOUISIANA CUISINE: Its 650 recipes helped make it the first real "textbook of Louisiana cuisine." The Junior League of Baton Rouge has printed nearly two million copies since 1959. Its Spinach Madeleine recipe is an all-time favorite of mine and countless others. (I've featured it on page 138.)

THE GASPARILLA COOKBOOK: The Junior League of Tampa released this in 1961, and it caused a stir for being a delicious melting pot of Southern, Greek, Cuban, Italian, and other recipes—all 712 of them—promoting the region's rich diversity.

THE COTTON COUNTRY COLLECTION: With that iconic tan-and-green illustration of a man gliding a pirogue down a bayou by a plantation home, this book, first published by the Monroe, Louisiana, Junior League in spiral-bound form in 1972, spills over with 1,156 recipes from across the state. The cake recipes are especially good.

A COOK'S TOUR OF MISSISSIPPI: Published by the *Clarion-Ledger* newspaper in 1980, this was a unique undertaking at the time. It features an intro by Willie Morris, thoughts from author Eudora Welty, exceptional documentary photography, and the state's most legendary recipes (including some from my grandmother, known as "Aunt Freddie," whose jellies and preserves were favorites of many, including Bob Hope and Lucille Ball).

STOP AND SMELL THE ROSEMARY: RECIPES AND TRADITIONS TO REMEMBER FROM THE JUNIOR LEAGUE OF HOUSTON: OK, so this 1996 book isn't spiral-bound; on the contrary, it was one of the first books of its genre to break out of a spiral shell and move into perfect binding, with lovely photography to boot. Many of the 500 recipes are still stellar for entertaining.

TABLES OF CONTENT: SERVICE, SETTINGS AND SUPPER: This 2006 book isn't spiral-bound either. But, like *Stop and Smell the Rosemary*, it's beautifully designed (in this case with a more contemporary look), with 350 recipes (some of them from renowned chefs) and an intro by Alabama native son and Pulitzer Prize winner Rick Bragg. (See its Walnut Stilton Torta, page 94.)

Homespun Chicken Pot Pie

SERVES 6–8

This is a recipe adapted from one that my dear friend and fellow Mississippian Paige Porter Fischer takes to anyone and everyone in need—"newlyweds too over the moon for each other to know what to cook, sleep-deprived new moms, or friends and family grieving a loss," she says. "It makes everyone feel warm inside." I couldn't agree more.

ONE 17.3-OUNCE PACKAGE FROZEN PUFF PASTRY SHEETS, THAWED

EGG-WHITE WASH (SEE PAGE 36)

⅓ CUP BUTTER

3 CUPS SLICED FRESH MUSHROOMS

1 CUP THINLY SLICED CELERY

1 CUP PEELED, SLICED CARROTS

1 CUP CHOPPED WHITE OR YELLOW ONION

½ CUP ALL-PURPOSE FLOUR

2 CUPS CHICKEN BROTH

1¼ CUPS HALF-AND-HALF OR CREAM

3 CUPS DICED COOKED CHICKEN

1 CUP FROZEN ENGLISH PEAS, THAWED

1 TABLESPOON DIJON MUSTARD (OPTIONAL)

1 TABLESPOON MINCED FRESH OR 1 TEASPOON DRIED THYME

½ TEASPOON GROUND BLACK PEPPER

¼ TEASPOON CELERY SEEDS

¼ TEASPOON GROUND SEA OR KOSHER SALT

4 TABLESPOONS CHOPPED FRESH PARSLEY

GARNISH: CHOPPED FRESH PARSLEY

1 Preheat the oven to 375°F.

2 Unfold a pastry sheet on a lightly floured surface. Roll the sheet into a 12-inch square.

3 Press the pastry into a 2-quart round dish, trimming any excess pastry. Prick the bottom and sides thoroughly with a fork. Brush with the egg-white wash and cover loosely with a layer of aluminum foil.

4 Bake for 25 minutes. Remove the foil and set the crust aside to cool.

5 In a large skillet, melt the butter over medium heat. Add the mushrooms, celery, carrots, and onion and cook for 4 to 6 minutes, stirring occasionally, until the vegetables are crisp-tender. Add the flour and stir for 3 minutes,

[CONTINUED]

or until the flour is golden brown. Slowly stir in the broth and half-and-half and let the mixture come to a boil. Allow it to thicken, stirring occasionally, about 2 minutes. (Add a little more flour to thicken the sauce even more, if necessary.)

6 Stir in the chicken, peas, mustard (if using), thyme, pepper, celery seeds, salt, and 3 tablespoons of the parsley. Remove the skillet from the heat.

7 Unfold the remaining pastry sheet on a lightly floured surface. Cut it crosswise into eight to ten 1½-inch-thick strips.

8 Spoon the chicken-vegetable mixture into the casserole. Weave a lattice pattern over the filling with the pastry strips and trim off any excess pastry. Sprinkle with the remaining 1 tablespoon parsley. Place the casserole on a baking sheet (which will catch any bubble-over and make it easier for you to remove the dish without touching it). Brush with more egg wash if desired.

9 Bake for 45 minutes, or until the filling is hot and bubbly and the pastry is golden brown. During the last 15 to 20 minutes of baking, cover the crust's edge with strips of aluminum foil to prevent excess browning. Garnish with more parsley before serving.

Storage
Tightly covered, this will keep nicely in the refrigerator for several days and in the freezer for up to 3 months. However, unlike most casseroles, because of its tender crust and creamy texture, to avoid sogginess this should go directly from the freezer to the oven without defrosting. See "Just Chill" (page 41) for more tips.

Jamie's Duck & Sausage Cassoulet

SERVES 8

This life-enhancing dish was created by the late and very great chef Jamie Shannon, one of the finest people you'd ever want to know. I got to know him while he was commanding attention for his impeccable skill and sincerity at Commander's Palace—Mecca for true New Orleans flavor and grace. Though Jamie passed away in 2001 at the much-too-young age of forty, he'd spent nearly half his life cooking at Commander's, and he is dearly missed. His culinary style leaned toward simple cooking that resulted in bold, rich, soul-satisfying fare, like this traditional and rustic French casserole, slow-cooked to sublime perfection. I toast to him each time I serve this—and hope you will too.

1½ POUNDS DRIED GREAT NORTHERN, WHITE NAVY, OR CANNELLINI BEANS

3 TABLESPOONS DUCK FAT (SEE NOTE) OR HIGH-QUALITY BUTTER

2 POUNDS FRESH SAUSAGE LINKS, CUT IN ABOUT TEN 4-INCH PIECES

1 POUND HAM HOCK

12 MEDIUM GARLIC CLOVES, MINCED

2 CUPS LARGELY DICED ONIONS

1 TEASPOON GROUND SEA OR KOSHER SALT

½ TEASPOON GROUND BLACK PEPPER

4 BAY LEAVES

½ TEASPOON FRESHLY GRATED OR GROUND NUTMEG

4 WHOLE DUCK LEG-THIGH QUARTERS (SEE NOTE)

6 SPRIGS FRESH THYME OR ROSEMARY

CRUSTY BREAD FOR SERVING

1 Wash the beans thoroughly in cold water, removing any debris; drain and set aside.

2 In a large heavy-bottomed pot over high heat, melt the duck fat. Add the sausage, ham hock, and garlic. Cook for 12 to 15 minutes, turning the sausage so that it's completely brown and the garlic is toasted. Keep a close eye on it and stir. Remove the meat from the pot and set aside.

3 Sauté the onions in the pot until they begin to get tender, about 5 minutes. Add the beans and cook for 3 minutes, stirring. Add 2 quarts water and season with the salt and pepper. Add the bay leaves and nutmeg and bring to a boil. Boil for 10 minutes, then reduce the heat, cover, and simmer for 1 to 1¼ hours, or until

[CONTINUED]

the beans are tender. (Don't overcook the beans or break them up by stirring. And don't let them burn on the bottom of the pan.) Adjust the seasoning as desired.

4   Preheat the oven to 350°F.

5   Using a slotted spoon, place about half of the beans in a large, wide earthenware dish or 5-quart cast-iron Dutch oven. Layer the sausage on top, then the ham hock, then the duck quarters, with one cut made into each leg and thigh. Place the remaining beans on top of the duck, reserving all of the leftover bean liquid. Place the thyme sprigs on top and pour over any leftover bean liquid or water, if needed, so that the liquid just reaches the top of the beans. Bake uncovered for 1 hour, or until the cassoulet comes to a simmer and a crust starts to form.

6   Reduce the heat to 250°F and cook for about 6 hours more, checking every hour to make sure the cassoulet is barely simmering. Whenever a crust has formed, gently push it down with the back of a spoon, allowing a new crust to form on top. As necessary, add enough bean liquid or water to moisten the beans.

7   After 6 hours, remove the cassoulet from the oven and let it rest for 20 to 25 minutes. Shred off the ham hock meat and discard the bone(s). Add the shredded ham back to the cassoulet. Garnish with thyme sprigs. Serve from the dish along with hearty, crusty bread for dipping into the sauce.

NOTE: Duck fat and duck quarters can be found at many gourmet markets or purchased online. You also can substitute 1 teaspoon of duck demi-glace for the duck fat. See Sources, page 167.

Storage

This dish tastes even better if you cook it, let it cool, then tightly cover and refrigerate it overnight. Remove the cassoulet from the refrigerator and let it sit at room temperature, covered for 1 hour. Reheat uncovered in a 350°F oven for 1 hour. Reduce the oven temperature to 250°F and let the cassoulet simmer, breaking up any crust that forms, for about 30 minutes, or until fully heated. Leftovers will freeze for up to 1 month, but since the consistency may be more soup-like, you may want to add some chicken broth to take it fully in that direction. See "Just Chill" (page 41) for more tips.

Nathalie's Overnight Biscuit, Sausage & Apple Casserole

SERVES 8

Charleston's Nathalie Dupree is the doyenne of Southern biscuit making, and I can promise you that once you try her Easy Cream Biscuits or any of the other baked goodness in her latest book, *Southern Biscuits*, you'll savor every morsel of her creativity. This breakfast casserole, made with her biscuits, is nothing less than divine. We all love biscuits and sausage, but may not have had them fancified in such a simple, beautiful way, with apples lending sparkle. This is a certified hit for breakfast, brunch, or dinner. Here's my adaptation, which includes a Dijon-cream sauce to serve either with the casserole (which really doesn't need it when it's fresh and moist from the oven) or with reheated slices of it (see Note).

2 POUNDS BULK MILD OR SWEET SAUSAGE

2 TART APPLES, CORED AND SLICED

1 RECIPE EASY CREAM BISCUITS (PAGE 36), TORN OR CUT INTO ½-INCH PIECES

3 CUPS MILK

2 CUPS GRATED SHARP CHEDDAR CHEESE

9 EGGS, BEATEN

1 TEASPOON DIJON MUSTARD

½ TEASPOON GROUND SEA OR KOSHER SALT

¼ TEASPOON GROUND BLACK PEPPER

DIJON-CREAM SAUCE (OPTIONAL FOR SERVING; RECIPE FOLLOWS)

1 Cook the sausage in a large skillet over medium heat, breaking it up as it cooks. Once it's crumbled and cooked through, use a slotted spoon to add it to a colander (leaving the drippings in the skillet) and allow it to cool.

2 Add the apples to the reserved fat over medium heat and cook until softened, 5 to 7 minutes. Remove them from the skillet and let cool in a small bowl.

3 Place the biscuit pieces in a large (at least gallon-size) zip-top plastic bag.

4 In a large bowl, whisk to combine the milk, cheese, eggs, and mustard. Stir in the sausage and apples. Season with the salt and pepper. Transfer the mixture to the

[CONTINUED]

plastic bag with the biscuits and seal it well. Place the bag inside another large resealable zip-top bag, opening in the other direction to prevent leaks. Refrigerate for at least 2 hours, but preferably overnight or up to 2 days. Lay it flat on a refrigerator shelf, occasionally turning it and massaging it to let the flavors come together.

5   When ready to bake, preheat the oven to 350°F.

6   Pour the mixture into a buttered 13-by-9-inch baking dish (or divide it between two 1½-quart or 8-by-8-inch casseroles in order to eat one and freeze the other). Break up any large pieces of sausage that may be in the dish.

7   Cover with aluminum foil and bake for 30 minutes. Uncover and bake for another 30 minutes, until the eggs are set and the center reaches 200°F. Serve immediately with the cream sauce, if desired.

NOTE: If you have leftovers, know that the biscuits will absorb a good portion of the liquid the longer it remains in the refrigerator, but here's what I like to do: Slice the casserole into squares, fry them in a skillet until well heated, and serve with the Dijon-cream sauce, which helps bring out the flavor of the sausage and apples beautifully, plus adds a touch of softness.

Storage
Cooked and stored in an airtight container, the casserole will keep in the refrigerator for up to 2 days and in the freezer for up to 2 months.

Dijon-Cream Sauce
MAKES ABOUT 1¼ CUPS

1 cup heavy whipping cream
¼ cup smooth or coarse-grain Dijon mustard
Ground sea or kosher salt
Ground black pepper

In a medium saucepan over low heat, combine the heavy whipping cream with the Dijon mustard. Whisk to combine until the mixture is thoroughly heated, about 4 minutes. Add a pinch or two of salt and pepper. This will keep in an airtight container for up to 2 days before using. Do not freeze.

Croque Monsieur
(French Ham 'n' Cheese) Casserole

SERVES 6–8

In late summer, just before school would start up, Nannie and Mama and I would take a weekend trip to New Orleans. Our mission? To let me shop for a few new outfits at the downtown Godchaux's Department Store—and have all of us leave with sated appetites. During a ladylike brunch at one of the French Quarter's classic restaurants, I was introduced to the *croque monsieur* (pronounced CROCK mesh-yeu), essentially an elegant French ham and cheese sandwich meant to be eaten with a knife and fork. Its beauty and rich flavor continue to captivate me. (Though I still stumble over its pronunciation.) I developed this brunch-perfect casserole to pay homage to that culinary discovery. *C'est si bon.*

TWO 8-OUNCE CANS REFRIGERATED CRESCENT DINNER ROLLS

¼ CUP DIJON MUSTARD

2 TEASPOONS FRESH LEMON JUICE

½ CUP GRATED PARMESAN CHEESE

3 CUPS GRATED GRUYÈRE CHEESE (SEE NOTE)

1¼ CUPS CLASSIC WHITE SAUCE (PAGE 24)

½ TEASPOON CHOPPED FRESH OR ⅛ TEASPOON DRIED THYME

⅛ TEASPOON GRATED NUTMEG

1 POUND THINLY SLICED BROWN SUGAR– OR MAPLE-GLAZED DELI HAM, TORN INTO ABOUT 3-INCH PIECES

GARNISH: FRESH THYME SPRIGS

1 Preheat the oven to 375°F.

2 Grease two 13-by-9-inch baking dishes. Unroll the crescent rolls into the dishes. Use your fingers to seal the perforations, pressing the dough up the dish sides so that it looks wavy and rustic. Bake each dish 10 to 12 minutes, or until the rolls are light golden brown. Remove the dishes from the oven and set aside to let cool.

3 In a small bowl, combine the mustard and lemon juice. Use a brush or spoon to spread half of the mustard-lemon

[CONTINUED]

mixture atop each of the hot, baked crusts. (It absorbs best when the crusts are still warm.)

4 Whisk the Parmesan and ½ cup of the Gruyère into the white sauce. Add the thyme and nutmeg and set aside.

5 Select the crust with the prettiest edging to use as the top and set aside.

6 In the dish with the bottom crust, spread half of the cheese sauce over the crust. Add the ham evenly across the crust and top with 1 cup of the Gruyère.

7 Remove the top crust from the other baking dish and place it atop the ham layer, using a wide spatula to press the top crust down gently. Evenly spread the remaining cheese sauce over it and top with the remaining 1½ cups Gruyère. Press down gently once more.

8 Bake for 15 to 20 minutes, or until the cheese is melted and the filling is thoroughly heated. If desired, turn the broiler to low and cook the casserole for 3 to 5 minutes, or until the topping is lightly browned in spots. Let cool 5 to 7 minutes and cut into squares. Garnish with thyme sprigs before serving.

NOTE: Suggested Gruyère substitutes are Emmentaler, Jarlsberg, or Swiss, in that order.

Storage

This can be made a few hours ahead of baking (but add the top layer of cheese just before putting it in the oven). Once cooked and tightly covered, it will refrigerate well for up to 3 days. I don't recommend freezing it because of its cream sauce and cheese, which could make it gummy once reheated. See "Just Chill" (page 41) for more tips.

Garden Lasagna in the Round

Wavy layers of wide noodles, creamy cheese, and herbed fresh vegetables never looked so elegant and tasted so good as in this well-rounded approach to standard lasagna. This is definitely a more refined way to showcase your farmers' market or garden's freshest offerings (and cooking prowess, of course). Though it's super-easy to make, it creates a picture-perfect presentation when served atop a cake stand (with extra marinara served in a pretty bowl to the side) at an outdoor brunch or early supper. Pour a good Pinot Noir with this and your guests will blush over it even more.

ONE 16-OUNCE BOX DRIED LASAGNA NOODLES (ABOUT 16; SEE NOTE)

2 TABLESPOONS OLIVE OIL

1½ CUPS GRATED CARROTS

1 CUP FINELY CHOPPED YELLOW SQUASH

1 CUP FINELY CHOPPED ZUCCHINI

2 TO 3 GARLIC CLOVES, MINCED

3 CUPS SLICED FRESH MUSHROOMS

TWO 6- OR 8-OUNCE PACKAGES PREWASHED BABY SPINACH

3 TABLESPOONS FINELY CHOPPED FRESH BASIL OR CHIFFONADE (SEE PAGE 43)

ONE 15-OUNCE CONTAINER RICOTTA CHEESE

½ CUP FINELY SHREDDED PARMESAN CHEESE

1 EGG, LIGHTLY BEATEN

½ TEASPOON GROUND SEA OR KOSHER SALT

¼ TEASPOON GROUND BLACK PEPPER

2½ TO 3 CUPS GO-TO MARINARA SAUCE (PAGE 27) OR ONE 24-OUNCE JAR TOMATO AND BASIL MARINARA SAUCE, PLUS MORE TO SERVE

2 CUPS SHREDDED ITALIAN CHEESE BLEND

GARNISH: FRESH BASIL SPRIGS

1 Preheat the oven to 375°F.

2 Cook the lasagna noodles in boiling water. Two minutes before their suggested cooking time, check to see if they're al dente (see "Use Your Noodle," page 31). If so, drain the pasta and rinse with cold water (to make them easy to separate). Drain the noodles again, this time laying them atop a wax paper–lined countertop.

3 Meanwhile, in a large skillet, heat 1 tablespoon of the olive oil over medium-high heat. Add the carrots, squash, zucchini, and half of the garlic. Cook and stir

[CONTINUED]

about 5 minutes, or until the vegetables are crisp-tender. Transfer the mixture to a large bowl.

4 Add the remaining 1 tablespoon oil to the skillet. Add the mushrooms and remaining garlic. Cook and stir 5 or 6 minutes, or until just tender. Gradually add the spinach and cook, stirring for 1 to 2 minutes, until the spinach is just wilted. Use a slotted spoon to drain the mushroom-spinach mixture before putting it into a medium bowl. Top with the basil and set aside.

5 In a small bowl, stir to combine the ricotta, Parmesan, egg, salt, and pepper. Set aside.

6 Spread ½ cup of the marinara in the bottom of a round 9-by-3-inch springform pan. Arrange 3 or 4 cooked noodles atop the sauce, overlapping and trimming them to completely cover the sauce as one layer, styling it so the noodle edges face the outside of each layer. Top with half of the vegetable mixture, half of the ricotta mixture, and half of the mushroom mixture.

7 Add another layer of 3 or 4 noodles. Evenly top with 1 to 1¼ cups marinara. Top with the remaining vegetable mixture. Sprinkle with 1 cup of the cheese blend.

8 Add another layer of 3 or 4 noodles. Layer with the remaining mushroom mixture and the remaining ricotta mixture.

9 Top with last layer of 3 or 4 noodles, 1 to 1¼ cups marinara, and the remaining cheese blend. Gently press down on the torte with the back of a spatula.

10 Place the pan on an aluminum foil–lined baking sheet. Cover the pan with a tented sheet of foil (so it won't touch the cheese) and bake for 40 minutes. Uncover and bake for 10 to 15 minutes more, or until heated thoroughly and the cheese is a light golden brown (use the broiler to get desired browning, if necessary). Cover and let the torte sit on a wire rack for 15 minutes before serving. Carefully remove the sides of the pan.

11 Cut the torte into eight wedges. Garnish with basil sprigs and serve with additional pasta sauce, if desired.

NOTE: I opted not to use no-boil lasagna noodles for this. No-boil noodles, especially ones made by Barilla, are often easy substitutes for traditional lasagna noodles, but the trick to using them is ensuring you have enough sauce to help them absorb moisture, and that said sauce covers every inch of the noodles. Since this torte is loveliest when its ruffled noodle ends are exposed, I avoided the potential of it having crispy edges.

Storage

This can be made up to 6 hours before cooking and kept refrigerated and tightly covered. Cooked and tightly covered, it will keep in the refrigerator for several days and frozen for up to 3 months. See "Just Chill" (page 41) for more tips.

Two-Bread Pudding with Honey-Bourbon Sauce

SERVES 8

I've had bread puddings galore, but none so beautiful as this one from the Fort Griffin General Merchandise Company Restaurant in Albany, Texas (near Abilene). The place is renowned for its steaks, but their bread pudding has been kept somewhat a secret. It's a chunky mix of light and dark breads—with the Bavarian being a nice nod to Texas' German heritage—and the silky-sweet sauce is, well, find out for yourself.

BREAD PUDDING

5 CUPS CREAM

3 EGGS, LIGHTLY BEATEN

¼ CUP SUGAR

1 TABLESPOON PURE VANILLA EXTRACT

1 TABLESPOON CINNAMON

1 TEASPOON GROUND NUTMEG

6 CUPS CUBED FRENCH BOULE OR SOURDOUGH BREAD

4 CUPS CUBED BAVARIAN OR PUMPERNICKEL BREAD

HONEY-BOURBON SAUCE

½ CUP UNSALTED BUTTER

1 CUP LIGHT HONEY

1½ OUNCES AMERICAN HONEY OR WILD TURKEY WHISKEY

TO MAKE THE BREAD PUDDING

1 Preheat the oven to 350°F.

2 Lightly grease a 13-by-9-inch glass baking dish.

3 In a medium bowl, whisk to combine the cream, eggs, sugar, vanilla, cinnamon, and nutmeg; set aside.

4 Lay 4 cups of the French bread cubes in the bottom of the prepared baking dish. Next lay the Bavarian bread cubes on top, then place the remaining 2 cups French bread on that. Use clean hands to mix up the middle and top layers to the desired appearance.

5 Pour the cream mixture over the bread. Gently press down on the bread to ensure that the pieces are covered with the cream mixture. Let the dish sit for 10 minutes, then cover it with aluminum foil.

[CONTINUED]

6 Bake for 20 minutes. Rotate the dish, uncover it, and bake it for another 20 minutes. When the pudding is set, remove it from the oven and set it aside to cool, loosely covered, for 30 minutes. Cover it tightly and place the pudding in the refrigerator to cool (and have the flavors meld) for at least 2 hours.

TO MAKE THE SAUCE

7 In a small saucepan, melt the butter over medium heat. Remove the pan from the heat and whisk in the honey, then the whiskey. Reduce the heat to low and cook the sauce for 2 to 3 minutes, until it's slightly thickened and thoroughly heated. Set aside. Cover to keep warm or let cool and refrigerate. Reheat over low heat in a small pan.

8 To reheat the pudding, place it in a 325°F oven and cook covered for 30 minutes, or until thoroughly heated.

9 Run a knife around the outer edge of the pudding before slicing it into squares. Serve each piece with 3 to 4 tablespoons of warm sauce.

Storage

Cooked and tightly covered, the bread pudding (with sauce stored separately) will keep in the refrigerator for up to 3 days and in the freezer for about 2 months. Just make a new batch of sauce while reheating any leftovers.

CHAFING DISH CHARM SCHOOL

Chafing dishes are smart and stylish containers for keeping your casseroles and party dips hot while you keep your cool. Here are the main things to know:

+ They work like this: A large (at least 4-quart) covered serving dish sits within a pan of water that fits within a raised frame. The bottom "steam" pan is heated by either cooking fuel (think Sterno) or electricity to keep food warmed at the proper temperature.

+ Chafing dishes are made to keep your casserole at a constant serving temperature—not to heat it up—so the food must be at the desired temperature *before* it goes in the dish (which itself should be hot before the food goes in). Make sure your food is cooked to 160°F beforehand and stays at that temperature after it's in the steam pan. If food gets below 140°F, you'll encourage bacteria to pay it—and your guests—a visit. If it gets above 160°F, you risk scorching it.

+ Fill the steam pan with hot water close to, but not touching, the food pan above to ensure the hot water stays at least 1½ inches beneath the food. Check the water level periodically to ensure it's adequate.

+ Cooking fuel, a nontoxic and biodegradable mix of alcohol, water, and gel, burns for about 2 hours, which is the maximum length of time a dish of food should stay out anyway.

+ Fuel canisters, available from hardware and party supply stores, can go into action once you remove the lid from the canister, slide it into the round space beneath the pan, and light the wick with a barbecue lighter.

+ New 4-quart chafing dishes run about $40, but vintage ones, which often are much more decorative, can be half that cost. They can also be rented from party supply stores.

+ Keep your dish tightly covered to retain heat and keep food moist.

+ Stir the food occasionally to ensure that food is warmed evenly.

+ For safety's sake, don't leave canister flames unattended, and once they burn out, allow them time to cool before attempting to remove them. (Fuel canisters now have labels to let you know they're safe to touch.) When removing the chafing dish cover, do so slowly to avoid burning yourself.

CHAPTER 04

Side Shows

When it comes to side dishes, we Southerners follow an important unwritten rule. For a special meal—be it a buffet for a crowd or a dinner for four—there should be at least two, preferably three, side-dish offerings. Why? They're not only a delight for everyone to behold, but they also keep your food's textures and flavors interesting while filling up the plate. In turn, that allows enough main-dish helpings (of say, chuck roast, baked chicken, fried catfish) to go 'round at least once. Most of us have learned this the hard way. You see, guests can go back for seconds, but if the "anchor" food disappears before everyone's had at it, you'll be in quite the pickle. Do yourself a favor: Don't risk it. Besides, everyone will love you to pieces for going the extra mile.

P.S. Since such side dishes as field peas, collard greens, or thick-sliced tomatoes are best simply prepared (i.e., not in casserole form), they aren't in this book. But they should indeed be one or two of your "extra" sides.

Divine Mac 'n' Cheese

Over the years that I've pursued macaroni-and-cheese perfection, this recipe has come pretty darn close to it. It's airy and elegant and just-right creamy, making you dream about any leftovers that might await in the refrigerator. The nutty, slightly salty flavor of Gruyère adds a sophisticated flavor that's irresistible.

1 POUND DRIED CAVATAPPI (SEE NOTES), ELBOW, OR PENNE PASTA	12 OUNCES GRUYÈRE, GRATED (SEE NOTES)	⅛ TEASPOON GROUND NUTMEG (SEE NOTES)
5 TABLESPOONS BUTTER	1 QUART HALF-AND-HALF	1 CUP PANKO OR PLAIN BREAD CRUMBS
	4 EGG YOLKS, LIGHTLY BEATEN	

1 Preheat the oven to 325°F.

2 Cook the pasta in boiling water. Two minutes before its suggested cooking time, check to see if it's al dente (see "Use Your Noodle," page 31); if so, drain the pasta (but don't rinse it with water).

3 In a medium bowl, melt 3 tablespoons of the butter in a microwave on defrost for 1 to 1½ minutes, until just melted. Set aside to let cool slightly.

4 Set aside ½ cup of the Gruyère. Put the rest in a large bowl. Add the half-and-half, egg yolks, melted butter (reserving that bowl for the next step), and nutmeg; whisk to combine well. Add the pasta and stir to thoroughly combine.

5 Using the same butter bowl, melt the remaining 2 tablespoons butter on defrost for 1 minute, until just melted. Add the bread crumbs and combine well.

6 Add the macaroni and cheese mixture to a greased 3-quart casserole dish. Top with the reserved Gruyère and sprinkle with the buttery bread crumbs.

7 Coat aluminum foil with nonstick spray. Cover the casserole, with the spray side facing down. Bake for 30 minutes. Uncover and cook for 15 to 20 minutes more. If the macaroni isn't golden enough, use the broiler set to low to brown it and watch closely for the desired appearance. Let it stand for at least 10 minutes before serving.

[CONTINUED]

NOTES: Elbows may be more traditional, but cavatappi (see Sources, page 167) are double elbows—with *rigati*, or grooves that help the sauce cling better—and thus, double the fun.

Gruyère substitutes are Emmentaler, Jarlsberg, or Swiss, in that order. Use a food processor to grate the cheese; otherwise it will take forever—and a bandage or two.

I think the Gruyère adds just the right amount of saltiness to this dish, but if you find this lacking in salt, please make amends.

Replace the nutmeg with a heaping ¼ teaspoon dry mustard (or more to taste) for a more traditional mac 'n' cheese. Add a pinch of cayenne pepper for even more kick. And substitute sharp Cheddar cheese for the Gruyère.

Storage

This can be made 1 day in advance; don't add the final layer of cheese and bread crumbs until just before baking. Cooked and tightly covered, this will keep well in the refrigerator for up to 3 days or in the freezer for up to 1 month. (If the pasta mixture gets too dry, add a bit more half-and-half and mix well before reheating.) See "Just Chill" (page 41) for more tips.

LIL' DISH

MAC 'N' CHEESE 'N' . . .

These precooked add-ins go together beautifully with mac 'n' cheese. Simply fold these ingredients into the pasta mixture before baking the casserole. Meat should always be precooked before adding, and most vegetables sautéed until just tender. Cooked seafood should be added in the last 10 minutes of baking so it'll stay soft and cuddly.

- Shrimp, crabmeat, or lobster
- Seasoned cooked hamburger or ground turkey
- Sliced or crumbled cooked sausage
- Pancetta or country ham
- Diced ham
- Crisp bacon crumbles
- Sautéed mushrooms
- Asparagus pieces
- Chopped broccoli
- Roasted red peppers
- Roasted green chiles
- Diced tomatoes or sliced Romas
- Pico de gallo
- Sliced green onions
- Basil or sage chiffonade (see page 43)

Bestest Cheese Grits Soufflé

SERVES 8–10

This takes some work on the front end to get and make traditional stone-ground grits, but the finished product will elicit unending superlatives from your dining companions. This pairs beautifully with pork (chops or sausage), seafood (especially barbecued or other garlicky shrimp), or as a hearty addition to a vegetable plate. And I say "bestest" here because that's how my family would describe the very best of the best—which really it is.

3 CUPS WHOLE MILK

1¾ CUPS COARSE STONE-GROUND WHITE GRITS (SEE PAGE 32; SEE NOTE)

3 CUPS GRATED SHARP CHEDDAR CHEESE

4 TABLESPOONS BUTTER

GROUND SEA OR KOSHER SALT

½ TEASPOON HOT SAUCE OR PINCH OF CAYENNE PEPPER (OPTIONAL)

6 EGGS, SEPARATED

1 Place electric-mixer beaters in a medium metal mixing bowl and put them in the refrigerator. Store there until ready for later use.

2 In a large nonstick saucepan, combine the milk and 2½ cups water over medium heat; bring to a boil (but watch the pot closely to ensure the liquid doesn't boil over). Slowly whisk in the grits, reduce the heat to medium-low, and cook for 10 minutes, stirring constantly. (The mixture will thicken and become difficult to stir with a whisk.)

3 Reduce the heat to its lowest level before adding a tightly fitting lid. Cook the grits for 20 to 40 minutes (depending on the fineness to coarseness of the hominy grain), using a wooden spoon to stir and scrape down the sides every 8 to 10 minutes, until the grits are creamy and tender.

4 Preheat the oven to 400°F.

[CONTINUED]

5 Pour the grits into a large bowl and let them cool for several minutes. Add the cheese, butter, 1 teaspoon salt, and hot sauce (if desired); mix well to combine. Stir in the egg yolks, one at a time, and combine well.

6 Remove the metal bowl and beaters from the refrigerator. Add the egg whites and a pinch of salt to the bowl. Beat the egg whites until stiff peaks form, about 7 minutes.

7 Add one-fourth of the beaten whites to the grits mixture and gently combine. Repeat three more times, until all the whites are folded into the grits. Pour the mixture into a greased 2½-quart soufflé dish and ensure that the top of the grits mixture is level and smooth.

8 Bake for 45 to 55 minutes, or until golden and set, which will be wet but jiggly. (Note that the soufflé will do most of its rising during the last 15 minutes of cooking, so keep it undisturbed while it does its thing.) Serve immediately.

NOTE: To save on time, this can be made with quick-cooking grits, but the texture won't be as refined, meaning that instead of achieving an airy soufflé (the true beauty of this dish), you'll get something akin to somewhat-fluffy baked grits. To substitute, bring 3 cups milk, 2 cups water, and ½ teaspoon salt to a boil in a medium, lidded pot. Add 1¼ cups quick-cooking grits and stir well. Reduce the heat to low, cover, and cook for 5 to 7 minutes, or until the grits are thickened.

Storage

This will keep well in an airtight container in the refrigerator for up to 4 days and in the freezer up to 2 months. I think the texture of frozen and reheated grits is compromised, but some of my friends swear they don't notice it.

Lilly's Sweet Onion Pudding

SERVES 8

You're welcome. I say this now because when you share this rich savory pudding, those on the receiving end will instantly proclaim you a god or goddess. For that we must all thank chef Kathy Cary of Louisville. The style of her dark-swanky-cozy restaurant, Lilly's—A Kentucky Bistro, is a throwback to old supper clubs, but its food is very much in the now. Kathy keeps her local, seasonal fare elegantly simple to showcase an ingredient's flavor to the max. This is especially wonderful paired with lamb or beef and also grilled vegetables.

2 CUPS CREAM

¾ CUP SHREDDED PARMESAN CHEESE

6 EGGS

3 TABLESPOONS ALL-PURPOSE FLOUR

1 TO 2 TABLESPOONS SUGAR (SEE NOTE)

2 TEASPOONS BAKING POWDER

1 TEASPOON GROUND SEA OR KOSHER SALT

½ TEASPOON CAYENNE PEPPER

¼ TEASPOON GRANULATED GARLIC

½ CUP BUTTER OR MARGARINE

6 SWEET ONIONS, VERY THINLY SLICED

1 In a large bowl, combine the cream, cheese, and eggs.

2 In a smaller bowl, combine the flour, sugar, baking powder, salt, cayenne, and granulated garlic. Gradually stir them into the egg mixture. Set aside.

3 Melt the butter in a large skillet over medium heat; add the onions. Cook, stirring often, for 30 to 40 minutes, or until the onions are caramel colored and fragrant. Remove from the heat.

4 Preheat the oven to 350°F.

5 Lightly grease eight 12-ounce ramekins or a 13-by-9-inch baking dish.

6 Stir the onions into the egg mixture, then spoon the mixture into the prepared dish(es) set atop a rimmed baking sheet.

7 Bake for 20 to 30 minutes, or until the pudding is set. (Ramekins will need the lesser amount of time.) Let stand 5 minutes before serving.

NOTE: Adjust this according to the sweetness of the onions; you may want the pudding sweeter or more oniony.

Storage

This will keep well in an airtight container in the refrigerator for up to 4 days. I don't recommend freezing.

LIL' DISH

HOW SWEET: THE SOUTH'S ONIONS

The South's War between the Sweet Onions got its start back in 1898 when a packet of onion seeds from Bermuda was planted in Cotulla (halfway between San Antonio and Mexico) in South Texas. With the success of Texas' crop of Bermuda onions, which are sweet and mild, other states followed suit. In 1931, using Texas' Granex variety (a yellow Bermuda hybrid), Georgia farmer Mose Coleman planted the seeds and was met with surprise: His onion was a lot sweeter than the ones in Texas, thanks to a unique blend of soil and climate in the southeastern region of his state. What resulted would soon be called the Vidalia onion based on where they had first been sold in a popular farmers' market.

Mose's curiosity paid off in the form of a global multi-multi-million-dollar business in Georgia. But Texans, not to be outdone, have been fighting for a piece of that pie. In 1986, plant geneticist Leonard Pike at Texas A&M developed the 1015 (named for its suggested planting date of 10-15). It was nicknamed the "million-dollar baby" because of the money invested in creating it. Many think it's a lot sweeter than the Vidalia. You be the judge.

River Road Spinach Madeleine

SERVES 4–6

Northerners release their inner pushiness at tag sales—Southerners at party-food and drink stations. Besides the bar, of course, a fancy fete's smorgasbord is where one can expect to find the grandest of chafing dishes, the most sparkling silver platters, the loveliest heirloom china casseroles—and a steely resolve to be fed. "Excuse me, I didn't see you were in line, I was so busy talking," a brassy socialite might say while cutting in front of you, plate firmly in tow. "I'll just scoot in here, honey. Now tell me who *you* are." This beloved casserole, served either as a side dish or appetizer, is almost certainly there vying for everyone's attention, especially in Louisiana and the states surrounding it. This recipe is adapted from one of my all-time favorite cookbooks, *River Road Recipes: The Textbook of Louisiana Cuisine*, by the Junior League of Baton Rouge (see page 107). It's excellent in stuffed tomatoes and tossed with pasta.

TWO 10-OUNCE PACKAGES FROZEN CHOPPED SPINACH, THAWED

¼ CUP BUTTER

2 TABLESPOONS ALL-PURPOSE FLOUR

2 TABLESPOONS CHOPPED ONION

½ CUP CREAM

1 TEASPOON WORCESTERSHIRE SAUCE

½ TEASPOON CELERY SALT

½ TEASPOON GARLIC POWDER

½ TEASPOON GROUND BLACK PEPPER

¼ TEASPOON GROUND SEA OR KOSHER SALT

1 CUP COARSELY CHOPPED PEPPER JACK CHEESE

¼ CUP ROASTED SWEET RED PEPPERS, DRAINED AND CHOPPED (OPTIONAL)

CAYENNE PEPPER (OPTIONAL)

GARNISH: CRUMBLED BUTTERY CRACKERS (CLUB OR RITZ)

1 Preheat the oven to 350°F.

2 Cook the spinach according to the package directions; drain it well (using paper towels if necessary) while reserving ½ cup of its liquid ("pot liquor"). Set aside.

3 Melt the butter in a large saucepan over low heat. Add the flour, stirring just until blended and smooth, about 2 minutes (do not let it brown). Add the onion and cook until soft, about 2 minutes. Add the cream and spinach liquor slowly, stirring constantly to avoid lumps.

4 Cook until smooth and thick, about 4 minutes. Add the Worcestershire, celery salt, garlic powder, black pepper, and salt; stir to combine. Add the cheese and the roasted red peppers and cayenne (if using). Stir until the cheese is melted and well combined, about 3 minutes. Add the spinach and stir well to combine.

5 Spoon the mixture into a 1½-quart casserole dish; cover and bake for 20 minutes. Uncover and bake for 5 minutes more, until the casserole is heated through and bubbly. Garnish with cracker crumbs before serving.

NOTES: To ensure this dish has the fullest-bodied flavor, you actually have to make it one day in advance. That frees up more time to primp and polish yourself and your home before a gathering. Now *that's* a party favor.

For a seductive appetizer, add 1 pound of jumbo lump crabmeat or crawfish tails just before serving. Stir well and keep warm in a chafing dish. (For more on using those, see page 126).

Storage

This should be cooked 1 day in advance before serving or sharing in a chafing dish. Cooked and tightly covered, it will keep well in the refrigerator for up to 3 days and in the freezer (without cracker crumbs) for up to 3 months. See "Just Chill" (page 41) for more tips.

Dempse's Dirty Rice

As my grandmother aged into frailty and my mother gave up any pretense that she could cook, our family feasts transitioned to my brother's house in Natchez, Mississippi. Like many Southern men (including our cousin, the late, great entertaining guru Lee Bailey), Dempse Bailey McMullen can cook. One dish he often made—a magnanimous accompaniment to Thanksgiving turkey and gravy—was a tribute to our late grandfather, "Pop," who before Dempse was the chief maker of this. You're more apt to hear it called "Cajun rice" as you get farther away from the Gulf, but in our neck of the piney, then swampy, woods, it's called "dirty rice." That's clean white rice "dirtied" with a swarthy mix of bacon, organ meats, and pork and/or beef, then kicked into high gear with jalapeños, garlic, and hot sauce. Yes, Dempse and I are still alive to tell the tale—and make this at least once a year.

4 BACON SLICES, CHOPPED

1 CUP CHOPPED ONION

½ CUP CHOPPED GREEN BELL PEPPER

¼ CUP CHOPPED CELERY

3 GARLIC CLOVES, CHOPPED

1 TO 2 JALAPEÑOS, SEEDED AND MINCED

1 POUND MIXED CHICKEN LIVERS AND GIZZARDS (OR OTHER MIX OF GIBLETS), TRIMMED, RINSED, AND GROUND OR CHOPPED (SEE NOTE)

1 POUND GROUND PORK AND/OR BEEF

1 TO 1½ TEASPOONS CAJUN SEASONING

½ TEASPOON GROUND BLACK PEPPER

¼ TEASPOON GROUND SEA OR KOSHER SALT

4 CUPS COOKED LONG-GRAIN RICE

¼ CUP CHOPPED GREEN ONIONS (WHITE AND LIGHT GREEN PARTS)

HOT SAUCE FOR SERVING

GARNISH: GREEN ONION SLICES

1   In a large cast-iron skillet, cook the bacon over medium heat for about 8 minutes, until just cooked (not crisp). Remove it to a paper towel–lined plate, leaving the drippings behind; set aside.

2   To the bacon drippings, add the onion, bell pepper, and celery, cooking over medium heat until softened, 5 to 7 minutes. Add the garlic and jalapeño and cook for 2 minutes more, until they begin to soften.

3   Add the liver, gizzards, and pork and cook until the meats are cooked through and lightly browned, 8 to 10 minutes. Add the Cajun seasoning, pepper, salt, and reserved bacon. Reduce the heat to medium-low and cover the skillet; let the mixture cook for about 20 minutes, stirring often.

4   Add the rice and green onions to the skillet, and stir to combine. Reduce the heat to low, re-cover the pan, and cook for 15 minutes longer, stirring occasionally, until the mixture's flavors have melded from steaming. Adjust the seasonings as desired. Serve with hot sauce and garnish with green onions.

NOTE: If the idea of livers and gizzards doesn't whet your appetite, just add more beef and pork (or better yet, the combination of the two to keep the flavors interesting). For a Creole version, add 2 cans diced Ro*Tel tomatoes with green chiles and one 8-ounce can tomato sauce.

Storage

This very moist rice dish tends not to freeze well; it turns to mush upon reheating. However, friends tell me that using brown rice keeps this in better freezer form, so I'm keen on giving that a shot next time I make this. See "Just Chill" (page 41) for more tips.

CREOLE OR CAJUN?

Renowned Louisiana chef John Folse has an encyclopedic knowledge of Cajun and Creole cooking. So much so that his 842-page tome on those very subjects, aptly titled the *Encyclopedia of Cajun & Creole Cuisine*, is a culinary tour de force. The beautifully designed and photographed book is written with a deep respect for both styles, which share strong French influences, but in different ways.

CREOLE FOOD = CITY FOOD. First documented in 1702 in Mobile, Alabama, Creole cooking reflects "a rich array of courses with close ties to European aristocracy," Folse says. The cuisine began developing around 1718 in New Orleans, where Native American, French, Spanish, English, African, German, and Italian cultures creatively mingled (and ultimately inspired the opening of America's first cooking school). Creole food incorporates traditional and refined French cooking techniques, delicate seafoods other than shellfish (think pompano), more variety of seasonings, and cream- and tomato-based sauces. For example, Creole gumbo's tomato base, heavily influenced by French bouillabaisse, is more delicate and soup-like than the Cajun version.

CAJUN FOOD = COUNTRY FOOD. Cajun cooking is a marriage of French country fare with the indigenous foods of South Louisiana swamps and bayous. It took root in 1755, when weary but rugged French exiles made it to friendlier terrain after the British expelled them from "Acadie" (Canada's Nova Scotia, New Brunswick, and Prince Edward Island) during the French and Indian War. The "Acadian" (shortened to "Cajun") cooking style underscores "their ingenuity, creativity, adaptability, and survival," Folse says. "They were happy to live off the land, which was abundant with fish, shellfish, and wild game." Cajun gumbo, for instance, is thickened with ground sassafras leaves (filé powder), which the Mi'kmaq indigenous people in Canada taught the Acadians to use.

Nannie's Cornbread Dressing

SERVES 10-12

Oh, if only one Freddie Jimerson Bailey had written this down for me. But Nannie didn't. So I had to test this umpteen times to get it to where I think she'd be pleased. She didn't use sugar in her cornbread, but in case you like it sweeter, I've included an option for it. Make the cornbread one day before, crumble it, and let it sit out in a bowl, loosely covered, so that it gets a bit stale in texture. That will help give it heft. And if you haven't noticed, we Southerners call it "dressing" and serve it on the side, thank you very much. Why? "Stuffing" is a more, well, indelicate word . . . and technique.

SKILLET CORNBREAD

¼ CUP BACON GREASE (FROM ABOUT 12 BACON SLICES) OR SAFFLOWER OIL

1 CUP YELLOW CORNMEAL

1 CUP ALL-PURPOSE FLOUR

4 TEASPOONS BAKING POWDER

1 TEASPOON GROUND SEA OR KOSHER SALT

½ TEASPOON SUGAR (OPTIONAL)

1½ CUPS WHOLE MILK, OR MORE IF NEEDED

1 EGG, LIGHTLY BEATEN

DRESSING

2 CUPS CUBED, LIGHTLY TOASTED OR STALE FRENCH BREAD

1 CUP COARSELY CHOPPED PECANS, TOASTED (SEE PAGE 45)

¼ CUP FINELY CHOPPED FLAT-LEAF PARSLEY

1 TABLESPOON GROUND SEA OR KOSHER SALT

1 TEASPOON GROUND BLACK PEPPER

½ TO 1 TEASPOON DRIED THYME

½ TO 1 TEASPOON DRIED SAGE

¼ TEASPOON CAYENNE PEPPER

8 TABLESPOONS BUTTER, OR MORE AS NEEDED

1½ CUPS CHOPPED GREEN BELL PEPPER

1½ CUPS CHOPPED ONION

1½ CUPS CHOPPED CELERY

½ CUP THINLY SLICED GREEN ONIONS (WHITE AND LIGHT GREEN PARTS)

3 HARD-COOKED EGGS, COARSELY CHOPPED

2 EGGS, LIGHTLY BEATEN

4 CUPS CHICKEN BROTH, OR MORE AS NEEDED

GARNISH: CHOPPED FRESH PARSLEY

TO MAKE THE CORNBREAD

1 Add the bacon grease to an 8-inch cast-iron skillet. Place the skillet in the oven and preheat the oven to 400°F.

2 Mix the cornmeal, flour, baking powder, salt, and sugar (if using) in a bowl. In another bowl, whisk together

[CONTINUED]

the milk and egg, then stir them into the dry ingredients. (Add a little more milk if the batter is stiff.)

3 Carefully remove the hot skillet from the oven and, with equal care, swirl the sizzling grease around the pan to evenly coat the bottom and sides. Pour the drippings into the cornbread batter and mix to combine. Pour the batter into the hot skillet, smoothing it with a spatula.

4 Bake for 20 minutes, until the cornbread is set and golden brown. Crumble the cornbread and put it in a large bowl, loosely covered, for at least 1 day. (If making the cornbread to eat by itself, it should serve 6 to 8.)

TO MAKE THE DRESSING
5 Preheat the oven to 350°F.

6 Add the French bread, pecans, parsley, salt, black pepper, thyme, sage, and cayenne to the cornbread.

7 In a large skillet, melt 4 tablespoons of the butter and add the bell pepper, onion, celery, and green onions. Cook over low heat until tender, about 5 minutes. Add them to the seasoned bread mixture.

8 Carefully mix in the hard-cooked eggs, then the beaten eggs.

9 Use a microwave-safe measuring cup or bowl to melt the remaining 4 tablespoons butter before mixing it with the broth. Pour it over the dressing.

10 Spoon the dressing into a lightly greased 14-by-10-inch roasting pan and cover tightly with aluminum foil. Bake for 45 to 55 minutes, or until set. Garnish with parsley and serve hot.

NOTE: If your dressing is too dry after baking or before reheating, don't fret. Warm 2 tablespoons butter with ½ cup chicken broth and mix it into your dressing; repeat if necessary.

Storage
This can be made 1 day in advance; add more buttery chicken broth (see Note) to add more moisture before baking. Cooked and tightly covered, this will keep well in the refrigerator for up to 3 days. For best results, freeze it uncooked. See "Just Chill" (page 41) for more tips.

LIL' DISH

AMEN TO THE BIG THREE

Blessed be the culinary "holy trinity"—onion, celery, and bell pepper. This trio, with garlic sometimes replacing the bell pepper, serves as the base of nearly everything cooked down South, but especially along the Gulf Coast. If time isn't on your side, substitute the required "trinity" amount of fresh chopped vegetables with an equal amount of frozen, plus a few tablespoons more to compensate for the water content. I'm never without a few bags of seasoning blend (a diced mix of onion, celery, and bell pepper) in my freezer; with butter or oil, and sometimes flour, they can make just about anything happen.

Mama Lois' Squash Casserole

SERVES 8

"Everyone, and I mean everyone, asks me for this recipe," says my Birmingham friend Lisa Frederick. "I clipped it from a newspaper, tried it one day on a whim, and I've never made any other version of squash casserole since." It's *so* good, she notes, "My mother-in-law might banish me from the house if I showed up for Thanksgiving dinner without it." Lisa, a native of Georgia, is also fond of the fact that this dish comes from "Mama" Lois Heard, whose presence at Lanierland country music venue was legendary (see "'Mama' Knew Best," facing page). "Mama Lois" added pimientos and jalapeños to hers to give it a visual and flavorful kick. Lisa's toned-down version, while still rich and oniony, works in harmony with other side dishes instead of potentially hogging the microphone, so to speak.

---

2 POUNDS LARGE YELLOW SQUASH, COARSELY CHOPPED

½ CUP BUTTER OR MARGARINE, MELTED

3 CUPS PEPPERIDGE FARM HERB-SEASONED STUFFING MIX (SEE NOTE)

2 CUPS SHREDDED SHARP CHEDDAR CHEESE

ONE 10.75-OUNCE CAN CREAM OF CHICKEN SOUP

1 MEDIUM ONION, FINELY CHOPPED

1 CUP SOUR CREAM

GARNISH: CRUMBLED BUTTERY CRACKERS (SUCH AS RITZ; ABOUT 16)

---

1 Preheat the oven to 350°F.

2 Grease a 2-quart casserole dish and set aside.

3 To a Dutch oven, add the squash and enough water to cover it. Bring to a boil over high heat, about 10 minutes; reduce the heat to medium-low, cover, and let the squash cook about 20 minutes more, or until tender. Drain the squash well and transfer the cooked pieces to a medium bowl. Mash the squash well with a fork or potato masher, and drain again if necessary.

4 In a medium bowl, stir together the butter and stuffing mix until thoroughly combined.

5 Add the cheese, soup, onion, and sour cream to the squash. Add 2 cups of the stuffing mixture and stir to combine.

6 Spoon the mixture into the prepared dish. Sprinkle the remaining stuffing mixture evenly over the top. Bake for 30 to 40 minutes, or until bubbly and hot throughout. Garnish with cracker crumbs before serving.

NOTE: "Do not use any stuffing mix other than the specified Pepperidge Farm," Lisa says. "Nothing else even comes close." For this recipe, you'll use half of a 14-ounce bag (which has 6 cups of stuffing).

Storage

This can be made the evening before you plan to bake it; add the final layer of stuffing just before cooking. Cooked and tightly covered, this will keep well in the refrigerator for up to 3 days. Uncooked, it will keep in an airtight container in the freezer for up to 4 months; add the final layer of stuffing prior to baking the defrosted casserole. See "Just Chill" (page 41) for more tips.

LIL' DISH

"MAMA" KNEW BEST

Lois Bannister Heard was the mother of Brenda Jones, the manager of Georgia's Lanierland country music venue until it closed in 2006. For nearly three decades, at the end of Jot-Em-Down Road, "Mama Lois" cooked up a spread of Southern classics for the performers and crew at every show. The country music stars who played there (the likes of Merle Haggard and Conway Twitty) grew to love her, and soon began requesting favorites from *her* repertoire. The group Alabama, for instance, loved her banana pudding, while Mr. Twitty fancied her fried chicken. She died several years ago, but thanks to dishes like this ultra-rich, oozy-gooey, irresistible casserole, her legacy will live on.

SHRED OF TRUTH

Why does the cheese you shred at home melt so much better in your casserole than the commercially available preshredded kind? It doesn't have wood pulp. Seriously. If you see "powdered cellulose" in a store-bought cheese variety's ingredients, and most likely you will, it means the cheese has been treated with powdered wood pulp (the fine white coating you sometimes see on each shred), which serves as a moisture barrier to keep the shreds from sticking together. Food manufacturers point out that this natural product, approved by the U.S. Food and Drug Administration for use in small amounts, is flavorless and harmless; they also brag that it even contributes to your fiber intake and helps bulk up food without adding calories. That's all well and good, but if you want cheese that melts the best without any, um, interesting additives, shred your own.

So-Nice Broccoli-Rice Casserole

The only canned anything in this is evaporated milk—a condensed cream that, with finely chopped mushrooms, celery, onions, garlic, and fresh broccoli (imagine that!), serves as the base of this dish's magnetism. That's a really nice change of pace from making it with cream of mushroom soup. So is using Gouda instead of Cheddar (or that cheese sprayed from a can), and almonds instead of ye olde water chestnuts. Oh! And you can add 2 cups chopped cooked chicken or turkey to this and make it a main course. I'm certain this will be one of your go-to dishes for both making and eating at any social occasion.

4 CUPS FRESH BROCCOLI FLORETS (SEE NOTES)

½ CUP COARSELY CHOPPED SWEET ONION

½ CUP COARSELY CHOPPED CELERY

1 TO 2 GARLIC CLOVES, CHOPPED

1 CUP SLICED FRESH BUTTON MUSHROOMS

2 TABLESPOONS BUTTER

1 TO 2 TABLESPOONS FRESH LEMON JUICE

¼ CUP ALL-PURPOSE FLOUR

ONE 12-OUNCE CAN EVAPORATED MILK

½ TEASPOON GROUND SEA OR KOSHER SALT

⅛ TEASPOON GROUND WHITE PEPPER

2 CUPS COOKED LONG-GRAIN RICE

2 CUPS SHREDDED GOUDA CHEESE (SEE NOTES)

½ CUP LIGHTLY TOASTED SLICED ALMONDS (SEE PAGE 45; SEE NOTES)

1 Preheat the oven to 350°F.

2 In the bowl of a food processor, pulse the broccoli, onion, celery, and garlic a few times until finely chopped. Add the mushrooms and pulse a few more times to ensure all the vegetables are finely chopped (but not pureed).

3 In a Dutch oven, melt the butter over medium heat. Add the vegetables and lemon juice and sauté for 2 to 3 minutes, until the vegetables soften. Add the flour and stir well to fully incorporate, cooking another 2 minutes.

[CONTINUED]

4 Slowly whisk in the evaporated milk, salt, and pepper and stir until well combined. Use a wooden spoon or spatula to fold in the cooked rice and 1½ cups of the cheese and stir until well combined, about 2 minutes.

5 Lightly grease a 2-quart baking dish. Spoon in the broccoli-rice mixture and spread it evenly in the dish. Top with the remaining ½ cup cheese.

6 Cover and bake for 25 minutes. Uncover, add the almonds, and bake for another 7 minutes, or until the cheese is melted and the mixture is bubbly. (If desired, turn the broiler on low to get a more golden topping, but watch it closely to ensure the nuts don't burn.) Serve immediately.

NOTES: One 10-ounce package frozen chopped broccoli, cooked and drained, can be substituted, but it won't offer the "meatier" texture and bright taste of fresh broccoli.

Gouda's complex depth of flavor is rich, slightly sweet, and nutty; hence, the best substitutes are, in this order, Edam, Havarti, Muenster, mild Cheddar, Cheddar-Jack, or only if necessary, Monterey Jack, which has the same semisoft consistency but is comparatively nondescript in flavor. Avoid using smoked Gouda because it, along with sharp Cheddar, will overpower this dish's fresh vegetable flavor.

Instead of topping this with sliced almonds, you can use 1 cup toasted slivered almonds in the mixture, but I think adding the sliced ones near the end is much more attractive. Frankly, if you really want almond joy, you could have both slivered and sliced.

If the mixture becomes dry as the rice absorbs the liquid, add more milk before reheating.

Storage

This can be made the evening before you plan to bake it; just add the final layer of cheese and nuts before cooking. Cooked and tightly covered, this will keep well in the refrigerator for up to 3 days and in the freezer for up to 2 months (just add the final layer of cheese and almonds after defrosting and then baking). See "Just Chill" (page 41) for more tips.

Corn Casserole in a Jiffy

This super-easy corn-and-more-corn casserole, most often made with Jiffy mix (see "Sweet on Jiffy," facing page), translates to warm, yummy comfort. Versatility, too; I often use this to host chopped leftover vegetables. Since this is never more exquisite than when its exterior is a golden brown, I use a metal pan to ensure it gets that way. Double this to make a 13-by-9-inch casserole.

2 CUPS FROZEN OR ONE 15.25-OUNCE CAN YELLOW SWEET CORN, DRAINED

ONE 14.75-OUNCE CAN CREAMED CORN

1 CUP 2% GREEK YOGURT OR PLAIN YOGURT, SOUR CREAM, OR BUTTERMILK (SEE NOTE)

1 CUP SHREDDED SHARP CHEDDAR OR MONTEREY JACK CHEESE (OPTIONAL)

ONE 8-OUNCE BOX JIFFY CORNBREAD MIX

½ CUP BUTTER, MELTED

ONE 4-OUNCE CAN CHOPPED GREEN CHILES, DRAINED (OPTIONAL)

2 EGGS, LIGHTLY BEATEN

GARNISH: SHREDDED SHARP CHEDDAR OR MONTEREY JACK CHEESE (OPTIONAL)

1 Preheat the oven to 375°F.

2 In a large bowl, combine the sweet corn, creamed corn, yogurt, cheese (if using), cornbread mix, butter, chiles (if using), and eggs. Pour them into a greased 9-by-6-inch loaf pan/glass dish or 8-by-8-inch baking dish.

3 Bake for 45 to 60 minutes, or until the casserole is set and a toothpick inserted in the center comes out clean. Garnish with a handful or so of cheese atop the casserole during the last 10 minutes of baking, if desired. Let stand 5 minutes before serving.

NOTE: Plain, unsweetened Greek yogurt, which wasn't available in Southern supermarkets until recently, gives this a moister flavor and texture than sour cream.

Storage

Once cooked and then refrigerated, this can be easily sliced and reheated in a nonstick skillet. Tightly covered, this will keep well in the refrigerator for up to 3 days and in the freezer for up to 2 months. See "Just Chill" (page 41) for more tips.

SWEET ON JIFFY

Technically, Jiffy isn't Southern. But at the same time, it is. The little blue-and-white box of corn muffin mix produced by the Chelsea Milling Co. originated in 1930 in the south of Michigan, but in our South it has a cult following for both value and flavor. It's sweeter and more cake-like than the rustic cornbreads we're known for. And that's precisely why people either love it or don't. Growing up, I adored it, appreciating how its sweetness accentuated the flavor of the sweet corn. My grandmother, on the other hand, dismissed it as "Yankee corncake." (See her skillet cornbread recipe on page 143.) But when the opportunity to make corn casserole presented itself, I didn't have to twist her arm too much to use Jiffy. Over the years, I've developed more of a taste for traditional cornmeals and cornbreads, but when it comes to using Jiffy in this recipe—as common at potlucks as a bucket of chicken—count me in.

Dueling Casseroles

Some of you would just *dhyyyyhhh* if you had to suffer through a holiday meal without French-fried onion rings on your green bean casserole, or marshmallows atop your sweet potatoes. Meanwhile, others of you would just *dhyyyyhhh* if you found either of those casseroles awaiting you. There's no denying, however, that the classic and contemporary versions of these iconic holiday sides have their merits. But I can truly testify that all four of these recipes are in good taste. The classics? Well, we all know, or need to know, how to make what so many people expect and crave. The contemporary? Both recipes hail from Natchez, Mississippi, friend and acclaimed chef Regina Charboneau, chef de cuisine of the riverboat *American Queen* and owner of the charming bed-and-breakast inn Twin Oaks and author of *Regina's Table at Twin Oaks*.

Classic Sweet Potato Casserole

SERVES 10–12

This dish is based on my grandmother's recipe, which was sweet but not make-your-teeth-fall-out sweet—which is how many of my friends and family members like it. I don't fall into that category. So whenever I cook some newfangled version—one that (*gasp!*) omits the marshmallows and adds weird stuff like brandy or cranberries—my dinner guests don't argue about it, but snipes do arise. One friend, aiming to put an end to the foolishness, once said in all seriousness, "They don't call 'em *sweet* potatoes for nothin'."

5 POUNDS SWEET POTATOES, PEELED AND CUT INTO 1-INCH CUBES, OR FIVE 16-OUNCE CANS UNSEASONED MASHED SWEET POTATOES (SEE NOTE)

1 CUP PACKED BROWN SUGAR

½ CUP GRANULATED SUGAR

½ CUP HALF-AND-HALF

½ CUP UNSALTED BUTTER, AT ROOM TEMPERATURE

2 TEASPOONS PURE VANILLA EXTRACT

2 TEASPOONS GROUND SEA OR KOSHER SALT

1½ TEASPOONS CINNAMON

1 TEASPOON GROUND GINGER

½ TEASPOON GROUND NUTMEG

4 EGGS, LIGHTLY BEATEN

4 CUPS MINI MARSHMALLOWS

1 Preheat the oven to 375°F.

2 Lightly grease a 13-by-9-inch or 3-quart casserole dish.

3 If using peeled, cubed sweet potatoes, put them in a large pot and cover with cold water. Bring to a boil over medium-high heat.

4 Reduce the heat to medium-low and simmer for 15 minutes, or until very tender. Drain the potatoes in a colander and let them cool slightly. In a large bowl, mash the sweet potatoes until smooth (you can do this with a hand mixer or food processor, if desired).

[CONTINUED]

5 Add both sugars, the half-and-half, butter, vanilla, salt, cinnamon, ginger, and nutmeg to the mashed sweet potatoes and stir well to combine; adjust the seasonings as desired. Add the eggs and mix well.

6 Spoon the sweet potato mixture into the prepared casserole dish. Cover with aluminum foil and bake for about 40 minutes, until heated through.

7 Remove the casserole from the oven and gently stir the mixture to ensure even cooking. Sprinkle the marshmallows atop the casserole and return it to the oven, uncovered, to bake for 15 to 20 minutes more, or until the marshmallows are golden brown.

NOTE: Sweet potatoes can also be cleaned, pierced several times on each side with a fork, and baked on a foil-lined, rimmed baking sheet at 400°F for about 1 hour. Or they can be boiled whole for about 45 minutes, or until tender; remove the skins and mash the potatoes as directed in the recipe. Five 16-ounce cans of candied yams can be used instead of the unsweetened mashed sweet potatoes, but you will need to omit the brown sugar and adjust the granulated sugar to taste.

Storage

The basic sweet potato mixture (without marshmallows) can be made 1 day in advance; follow the baking directions, knowing you may need to cook the mixture 10 minutes more to thoroughly heat it if it goes in the oven very cold. Add the marshmallows during the last 15 to 20 minutes of cooking. Cooked and tightly covered, this will keep in the refrigerator for up to 3 days. This will not freeze well.

LIL' DISH

SWEET CONFUSION

No matter if you like your sweet potatoes more on the dessert side, or in a savory fashion, here's what we all need to agree on—though many of you will stay in denial about this: A sweet potato is not a yam. They're two different tuber species. So there. I've said it.

Here's what happened: When Africans arrived to this country, they recognized the sweet potato as being similar to the root vegetable native to their homeland, one they knew was good to eat. (*Yam* comes from an African word meaning "to eat.") To further confuse the issue, the USDA began distinguishing orangey-fleshed sweet potatoes from paler sweet potatoes by labeling the coppery ones "yams." But they just ain't so. And here's what you need to know:

SWEET POTATOES, native to North America, most often have light bronze skins with orange flesh. These are sweeter and moister than "white" sweet potatoes, which have a light golden skin and cream-colored flesh.

YAMS are common to Africa (West Africa grows 95 percent of the world's yams) as well as the Caribbean and Asia. They have a coal-colored, scaly skin with purple, reddish, or white flesh. They're starchier and blander than sweet potatoes, which is often why they're served with spicy sauces.

Sweet Potato Casserole with Candied Cranberries & Orange Zest

SERVES 6

The South's beloved sweet potato casserole (see page 157) loses its mainstay marshmallows but gains some fresh citrus appeal.

SWEET POTATO CASSEROLE

1¾ POUNDS SWEET POTATOES, PEELED AND CUT INTO 1-INCH CUBES

1 CUP PACKED BROWN SUGAR

½ CUP CREAM

½ CUP BUTTER, MELTED

2 EGGS, LIGHTLY BEATEN

¼ TEASPOON CINNAMON

CANDIED CRANBERRIES AND ORANGE ZEST TOPPING

1 CUP FRESH CRANBERRIES

1 ORANGE, ZESTED (SEE NOTE)

½ CUP GRANULATED SUGAR

¼ CUP WHITE BRANDY

TO MAKE THE CASSEROLE

1 Preheat the oven to 400°F.

2 Lightly grease a 1½- to 2-quart casserole dish.

3 Put the sweet potatoes in a large pot and cover with cold water. Bring them to a boil over medium-high heat. Reduce the heat to medium-low and simmer for 15 minutes, or until they are very tender. Drain the potatoes in a colander and let them cool slightly. In a large bowl, mash the sweet potatoes until smooth (you can do this with a hand mixer or food processor if desired).

4 Use an electric mixer to combine the sweet potatoes, brown sugar, cream, butter, eggs, and cinnamon; whip the mixture until smooth.

5 Spoon the mixture into the prepared casserole dish. Set aside.

TO MAKE THE TOPPING

6 Coat a rimmed baking pan with nonstick spray and add the cranberries and orange zest.

7 Sprinkle on the granulated sugar and drizzle the brandy over the cranberry mixture. Mix together well.

8 Put the sweet potato casserole in the oven with the baking sheet of cranberry-zest mixture and bake for 15 minutes.

9 Remove both the casserole and the baking sheet. Use a spatula to remove the cranberry-zest mixture and carefully sprinkle it atop the sweet potato casserole.

10 Reduce the oven temperature to 350°F.

11 When the oven reaches the reduced temperature, return the casserole to bake for another 10 minutes, until the mixture is set and the edges are light golden brown. Serve immediately.

NOTE: Use a zester to get at least 1-inch strips.

Storage

The sweet potato base and topping can both be made in advance and refrigerated, tightly covered, for up to 1 day. Cooked and stored in an airtight container, they will keep in the refrigerator for up to 3 days. I don't recommend freezing this.

Classic Green Bean Casserole

SERVES 8-10

Campbell's Soup introduced this recipe in 1955—and a crunchy, gooey culinary legend was born. French-fried onion rings aren't just for this one casserole. Consider adding them to just about any creamy casserole that could benefit from some crunch and onion flavor.

¼ CUP BUTTER

1 CUP SLICED FRESH MUSHROOMS

½ TO ¾ CUP FINELY CHOPPED YELLOW OR SWEET ONION

6 CUPS CHICKEN BROTH

8 CUPS FRESH OR FROZEN GREEN BEANS, 3 TO 4 INCHES LONG (SEE NOTES)

TWO 10.75-OUNCE CANS CREAM OF MUSHROOM SOUP (SEE NOTES)

1 CUP WHOLE MILK

1½ CUPS GRATED SHARP CHEDDAR CHEESE

2 TEASPOONS SOY OR WORCESTERSHIRE SAUCE

⅛ TEASPOON GROUND BLACK PEPPER

TWO 2.8-OUNCE CANS FRENCH-FRIED ONION RINGS

1 Lightly grease a 13-by-9-inch or 3-quart casserole dish; set aside.

2 In a Dutch oven, melt the butter over medium heat. Add the mushrooms and onion and sauté until tender, 5 to 7 minutes. Spoon the sautéed vegetables into a large bowl, reserving the drippings in the Duch oven.

3 Preheat the oven to 350°F.

4 Add the broth to the Dutch oven and bring it to a boil over medium heat. Add the green beans, reduce the heat to medium-low, cover, and cook until the beans are tender, about 10 minutes. Drain them in a colander and set aside.

5 To the large bowl with the onion and mushrooms, add the green beans, mushroom soup, milk, 1 cup of the cheese, the soy sauce, and pepper. Stir gently to combine; adjust the seasonings as desired. Let stand 5 minutes before serving.

6 Spoon half of the green bean mixture into the prepared dish. Top with 1 can of the onion rings. Add the remaining green bean mixture.

7 Bake uncovered for 30 minutes. Remove the casserole from the oven and top with the remaining onion rings and the remaining ½ cup cheese (or more, if desired). Bake an additional 10 to 15 minutes, until the casserole is bubbly, the onion rings are crisp, and the cheese is melted.

NOTES: Substitute two 16- to 20-ounce bags or two 9-ounce packages of green beans, if desired. If using canned (precooked) green beans, omit the cooking step (though the beans will be more flavorful if cooked fresh).

For more flavor, try the roasted garlic–flavored cream of mushroom soup.

Storage

Cooked and stored in an airtight container, this will keep in the refrigerator for up to 3 days. I wouldn't advise freezing the cooked casserole, but if you blanch the green beans (see directions for doing that in Green Bean & Artichoke Mornay Casserole, page 164), you can make the creamy green bean base (without adding the onion rings) and freeze it for about 1 month. Defrost it in the refrigerator and add the onion rings and final layer of cheese just before baking. See "Just Chill" (page 41) for more tips.

Green Bean & Artichoke Mornay Casserole

SERVES 8

If you're keen on that creamy classic (see page 162) that packs a crunch, you'll be over the moon for this uptown version. Here, crisp-tender green beans and chunks of artichoke hearts luxuriate in an immensely flavorful cheese sauce under freshly fried onion ringlets.

REGINA'S MORNAY SAUCE

2½ CUPS CLASSIC WHITE SAUCE (PAGE 24)

1 CUP GRATED GRUYÈRE CHEESE

½ CUP GRATED EMMENTALER CHEESE

¼ CUP CREAM

½ TEASPOON GROUND SEA OR KOSHER SALT

½ TEASPOON GROUND WHITE PEPPER

PINCH OF CAYENNE PEPPER

GREEN BEAN AND ARTICHOKE MIXTURE

GROUND SEA OR KOSHER SALT

8 CUPS FRESH, CUT GREEN BEANS (3 TO 4 INCHES LONG)

¼ CUP BUTTER

2 CUPS ARTICHOKE HEARTS, CHOPPED

¼ CUP FINELY SLICED OR MINCED GREEN ONIONS (WHITE AND LIGHT GREEN PARTS)

GROUND WHITE PEPPER

THIN FRIED ONION RINGS

VEGETABLE OIL

¾ CUP ALL-PURPOSE FLOUR

1 EGG

½ TEASPOON GROUND SEA OR KOSHER SALT

½ TEASPOON BAKING POWDER

1 LARGE SWEET OR YELLOW ONION, VERY THINLY SLICED INTO RINGS

TO MAKE THE SAUCE

1 In a medium saucepan, combine the white sauce with both cheeses. Cook over low heat until the cheeses are melted and the mixture is smooth. (Do not let it boil.)

2 Add the cream to a small microwave-safe dish and cook it on high at 1-minute intervals until it reaches 140°F.

3 Add the hot cream to the sauce mixture and season with the salt, white pepper, and cayenne; whisk to combine. Remove it from the heat and cover. Stir occasionally to keep smooth (reheating on low if necessary) while making the green bean and artichoke mixture.

[CONTINUED]

TO MAKE THE GREEN BEANS AND ARTICHOKES

4 Preheat the oven to 375°F.

5 Place a colander in a sink. Add 10 cups water with about 3 cups ice to a large bowl; place it either in or near the sink.

6 To a large pot, add 12 cups water and 1 teaspoon salt. Bring it to a boil over high heat. Carefully add the green beans and boil for 3 minutes. Test for tenderness (they should be tender but not soft), and, depending on their thickness, return to a boil for another 1 minute if necessary. Immediately (and very carefully) pour the beans into the colander to drain (keeping your face away from the hot steam). Just as quickly and carefully, pour the drained beans into the bowl of ice water. Let them stay there for 2 to 3 minutes before returning the beans to the colander to drain again.

7 In a large skillet, melt the butter over medium heat and sauté the blanched green beans, artichoke hearts, and green onions, until the mixture is well combined and heated through. Season with salt and pepper.

8 Lightly grease a 3-quart baking dish.

9 Add the green bean mixture to the prepared dish and top with the mornay sauce.

10 Bake uncovered for 25 minutes, until lightly browned.

TO MAKE THE ONION RINGS

11 In a large deep skillet or deep-fat fryer, heat vegetable oil (at least 1 inch deep) to 375°F.

12 In a medium shallow bowl, whisk to combine the flour, ¾ cup water, the egg, salt, and baking powder.

13 Dredge the onion rings in the batter and carefully place them into the hot oil. Cook, turning once, for 2 to 3 minutes, or until they are golden brown. Drain well on paper towels.

14 Garnish the casserole with the onion rings before serving.

Storage

Cooked and stored in an airtight container, this will keep in the refrigerator for up to 3 days. I wouldn't advise freezing this, since its freshness is what makes it superb (plus the sauce can break down, making it not suitable for a special occasion).

SOURCES

CASEROLE CARRIER BASKET
(shown on page 81)
Found online from Joanna's Collections:
Etsy.com/shop/joannascollections.

CAVATAPPI PASTA
Available at most large supermarkets, gourmet grocers, or online at PastaCheese.com or GourmetItalian.com.

CLEMSON BLUE CHEESE
Available at campusdish.com/en-US/CSSE/Clemson/BlueCheese or by calling 800-599-0181.

DUCK LEG-THIGH QUARTERS
Available at most gourmet markets or online from FarmFreshDuck.com / (610) 562-8482 or MapleLeafFarms.com / (800) 348-2812.

EMERIL'S SEASONINGS
Available at most large supermarkets, gourmet grocers, or online at EmerilStore.com.

FAT/DEMI-GLACE
FarmFreshDuck.com / (610) 562-8482 (fat only) or Dartagnan.com / (800) 327-8246 (fat and demi-glace).

LOUISIANA CRAWFISH
Available at most large supermarkets or online from CajunGrocer.com / (888) 272-9347; or LouisianasBestSeafood.com / (504) 464-9808.

ORGANIC LEMON, LIME JUICES
Available at most organic grocers or from Vitacost.com / (800) 381-0759

STUBB'S ROSEMARY-GINGER SPICE RUB
Available at most large supermarkets, including Walmart and Piggly Wiggly, or online at Amazon.com.

PAGE 36: EASY CREAM BISCUITS

adapted from *Southern Biscuits* (Gibbs-Smith, 2011) by Nathalie Dupree and Cynthia Graubart, used with permission from author Nathalie Dupree.

PAGE 57: SISSY'S SPICY SHRIMP & CHEESE GRITS

adapted from *Ladies' Legacies in Natchez* (Natchez Publishers, 2007) by Sissy Eidt and Mary Eidt, used with permission from author Sissy Eidt.

PAGE 62: SKILLET CATFISH-PECAN BAKE

adapted from a recipe by Delta Pride Catfish Inc. of Indianola, MS, used with permission from the company.

PAGE 94: WALNUT STILTON TORTA

adapted from one contributed by Susan Smith Ellard to the Junior League of Birmingham's *Tables of Content: Service, Settings and Supper* (Favorite Recipes Press, 2006), used with permission from the Junior League of Birmingham.

PAGE 100: SHRIMP & ARTICHOKE CASSEROLE BIENVENU

first published in the *Times-Picayune* newspaper by Marcelle Bienvenu, used with permission by author Marcelle Bienvenu.

PAGE 111: JAMIE'S DUCK & SAUSAGE CASSOULET

adapted from *Commander's Kitchen: Take Home the True Taste of New Orleans With More Than 150 Recipes from Commander's Palace Restaurant* (Clarkson Potter, 2000), by Ti Adelaide Martin and Jamie Shannon, used with permission from author Ti Adelaide Martin.

PAGE 115: NATHALIE'S OVERNIGHT BISCUIT, SAUSAGE & APPLE CASSEROLE

adapted from *Southern Biscuits* (Gibbs-Smith, 2011) by Nathalie Dupree and Cynthia Graubart, used with permission from author Nathalie Dupree.

PAGE 123: TWO-BREAD PUDDING WITH HONEY-BOURBON SAUCE

adapted from a recipe in *The Big Texas Steak House Cookbook* (Pelican Publishing, 2011), used with permission from its creator, the Fort Griffin General Merchandise Company Restaurant in Albany, TX.

PAGE 136: LILLY'S SWEET ONION PUDDING

adapted from one created by chef Kathy Cary of Lilly's—A Kentucky Bistro in Louisville, KY, used with permission from Chef Cary.

PAGE 138: RIVER ROAD SPINACH MADELEINE

adapted from *River Road Recipes: The Textbook of Louisiana Cuisine* (The Junior League of Baton Rouge, 1959), used with permission from the publisher.

PAGE 146: CRAWFISH DRESSING À LA JOHN FOLSE

adapted from a recipe in the *Encyclopedia of Cajun & Creole Cuisine* (Chef John Folse & Company Publishing, 2004), used with permission from the author.

PAGE 148: MAMA LOIS' SQUASH CASSEROLE

adapted from a recipe created by the late Lois Bannister Heard of Cumming, GA. Recipe and portrait (page 149) used with permission of her family.

PAGE 160: SWEET POTATO CASSEROLE WITH CANDIED CRANBERRIES & ORANGE ZEST AND PAGE 164: GREEN BEAN & ARTICHOKE MORNAY CASSEROLE

adapted from recipes in *Regina's Table at Twin Oaks* (Regina's Table Press, 2007), by Regina Charboneau, used with permission from the author.

INDEX

INDEX